INTRODUCTION

Jim Brennan had a dream. As a successful Colorado businessman, he was accustomed to realizing many dreams. This one, however, was of a whole different order. Jim Brennan wanted to build a sailing vessel and sail around the world.

Mermaid's Log is the true story of the adventures from her backyard construction in Ft. Collins, Colorado to circumnavigating the North Atlantic Ocean and then the world from 1988 to 1993. It contains an accurate account of what one can generally expect on a passage at proper seasons on each ocean. It also contains experiences of some fellow yachtsmen having close encounters with tragedy, survival, and theft. This is a learning experience.

Throughout the book you will enjoy the ***cruising information*** and going to ports of call. There is specific information on ***tactics to sail around South Africa***. You will read about many adventures and a unique love story. It tells of how Jim meets his future wife, Marione, a daughter of a very sheltered family, of how Marione, a totally inexperienced sailor, took a leap of faith in her love for him and joined the ***Mermaid*** to become an experienced, trusted, sailing partner, sharing in all the adventures and all the encounters. ***Jump aboard the Mermaid and lets go sailing.***

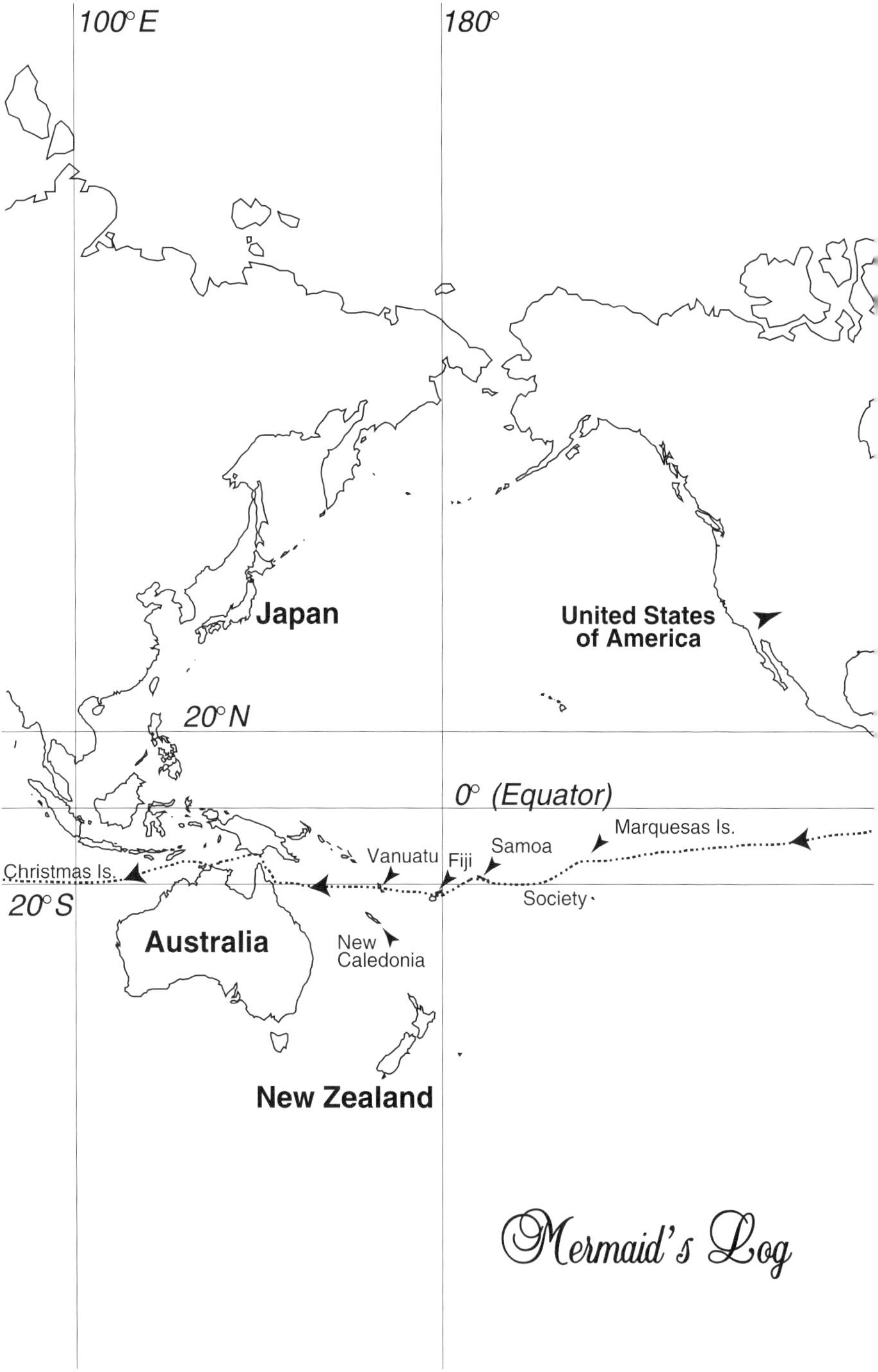

Mermaid's Log

40° W
N
W
E
S
Spain
Portugal
Azores
Bermuda
Maderia
Canaries
Cape Verde
Trinidad
Ecuador
Natal
Brazil
Destiny
(Meeting)
South Africa
Mayotte
Mauritius
Malagasy

GOOD LUCK

How can it be that I am in this great ocean of thee?

And see so many lovely things that are all free?

Wherever I look, wherever I am

In these great oceans I see them.

The graceful birds that glide away

The lovely fish that jump and play

All free and living day to day.

How lucky am I to be here and see them play.

Happy Sailing
go for it!

Mermaid's Log

Jim Brennan

Jim Brennan
Marione Bre[illegible]

11-03-07

MERMAID'S LOG

A True Adventure Story

By Jim Brennan

St Pete boat show

DISCLAIMER

This book is a true account and in every respect I have attempted to retain its accuracy. If I have made any errors I am not aware of them and I apologize. In addition, I assume no responsibility if any reader should follow the theories or suggestions expressed herein.

Published by James A. and Marione D.D.S. Brennan

To order this book from the author, send your order to telephone Fax number **941-696-8066.**

Library of Congress Catalog Card Number 96-96800

ISBN: 0-9652907-4-3

Composition, Printing and Binding by
Ralard Printers, Inc.
San Antonio, Florida
(352) 588-2800

Map Design by
Kenneth R. Alford
614 Royal Palm Avenue
Clewiston, Florida 33440-2917
(941) 983-3334

DEDICATION

To Marione, my wife, found by good fortune in Brazil. A better companion a man never had.

To my daughters, Lisa, Kristina, and Kelly, who watched Mermaid grow from a pile of wood to a sea boat and who scrubbed her deck many times.

To all the friends who helped me on ***Mermaid*** when building her. In particular, Bill Spooner, who helped fire my imagination to the task and gave his expertise whenever it was needed.

TABLE OF CONTENTS

POEMS

MAPS (Not for Navigation)

How to See a Green Flash

Page 31

Appendix:

THE CRUISERS

The cruisers come from the ban
On the land that have a dream
And are living it as best they can
They are people that can stand
And be self-sufficient off the land
Free from government and man
They make a plan
And set their sails and wail
Give me wind, man, so my machine can jam.

BUILDING THE MERMAID

• Keep It Simple

• Build It With Common Sense

• And Go Sailing

I built my yacht, Mermaid, in Fort Collins, Colorado, where I was living at the time. I had good advice and assistance from many friends. I started to pour the six thousand pounds of lead keel, outside ballast, on Christmas Eve, 1974. It was twenty degrees below zero-certainly no time to be pouring lead! My enthusiasm was so great that even weather wasn't going to slow down my progress!

Three days later, I was still chopping the lead back into small pieces to be remelted and repoured. It had been so cold that the lead did not fuse properly with each pour and ended up layered. This set back didn't destroy my desire to see the ***Mermaid*** floating. Persistence prevailed. With the help of various friends and their expertise when needed, ***Mermaid*** grew in my backyard until she was a fine-looking vessel. As she grew, I'd sit on the deck at sunset, thinking, "One day I will see sunsets like this from this deck on the oceans of the world!"

Mermaid is thirty-six feet long, twelve feet wide, and draws four feet, eight inches. She weighs fourteen tons. She is a sloop with ***three reefs*** in the main sail and three differently sized head sails. She has a Perkins 4-108 industrial engine rated at 50 horsepower and a capacity of one hundred and twenty-two gallons of diesel fuel. She carries two hundred gallons of water in four independent baffled tanks. She also carries eleven kilos of propane.

Building your own boat gives a certain freedom to make some minor changes in its design. I stretched the length three feet and modified the ship from a ketch to a sloop. I raised the below-deck headroom so that I can stand up straight everywhere. I also laid out the below-deck accommodations to my liking.

Mermaid's construction is of wood with fiberglass cloth covering the total exterior. I have found this combination to be very satisfactory over the last eighteen years and see no reason to change. I love wood, but hate the maintenance. Fiberglass eliminates this problem.

Mermaid's electronics consist of four tiller automatic pilots, a depth sounder, an automatic direction finder, a hand held VHF, and an ICOM 735 ham radio. There is also a TV and VCR for viewing movies. Her primary navigation system is a Plath sextant with Hydrographic Office 249 Air Navigation Tables Volumes I, II, and III. I also have a Simonson Junior back-up sextant.

All systems are accessible, basic, and easy to service or repair. The engine room is convenient to work in. Oil can be drained using the oil pan drain under the engine. All engine maintenance, including removal of the transmission, can be accomplished without moving the engine. The stuffing box is plainly visible and easy to get at for tightening or adjustment.

The two 6-volt, 225-amp, golf cart batteries, in series with water fill holes on top, provide electricity. A 12-volt, high amp cranking battery, independent of the main electrical system, is used to start the engine. An 80-amp Motorola truck alternator with a solid state regulator and a bypass rheostat serves as the charging system. A 1200-watt generator is also on board.

Mermaid's electrical capability is complemented by two, 40-watt, solar panels, which keep the battery voltage up at sea. These panels charge the battery sufficiently to carry the tri-light, tiller pilot, water pump, inside electric, radio reception, and limited ham radio communications. I reduced my amperage requirements when I threw my refrigerator overboard ten years ago.

Mermaid's compass is set on her lubber line (a fixed line on a compass aligned with the longitudinal axis of the boat) in a pedestal for protection. There are holes on top of the pedestal to enable setting a pelorus on the lubber line. This makes it possible to steer the ship to adjust the compass error out, east and west, and north and south, and also allows me to swing the vessel three hundred and sixty degrees to calculate a deviation table. All of this is done by using the azimuth (bearing) of the sun shown on the pelorus.

Mermaid's capability of being able to lower her mast independent of shore has proved to be very useful. With a low bridge, the mast can be tilted to an angle low enough to get under and continue on.

On November 20, 1977, ***Mermaid*** was completed. She sat on a borrowed lowboy behind my truck, ready for me to drive my baby to Corpus Christi, Texas for her introduction into the environment she was made for. What a grand view it was, as I drove down the road, to look into the rear view mirror and see this big, beautiful, seagoing machine rolling behind me to the adventures I had planned for us both, and for those who would join us along the way.

I arrived in Corpus Christi in the midst of a busy four-day Thanksgiving weekend. I found a man with a crane who had no reservations about working on a holiday weekend. His crane picked up the ***Mermaid*** before a gallery of about thirty spectators.We all cheered as she went into the water and sat parallel to the waterline. I had modified the basic plans to accommodate my desires and wasn't all that sure that I hadn't altered the design so much that the boat would be out of trim in the water and wouldn't sit parallel to the waterline. One never knows just exactly what will work until the boat is actually in the water.

Once ***Mermaid*** was in the water, a friend helped me to set up the hoisting arrangement on the mast which is stepped on a tabernacle. We winched up the mast and secured the rigging. Two hours after launching, the mast was standing.

Mermaid had been designed to put four thousand pounds of ballast inside, distributed equally throughout. I wondered if that was enough inside ballast to get her to the waterline. Because she sat so beautifully parallel with the water, though six inches too high, the inside ballast could be equally distributed to bring her down to the waterline. I was delighted to find that the ballast in place was heavy enough to do the job.

The next day, while the sail maker measured sails, I got all the internal systems going. The engine ran very well as I motored happily around the harbor. Once the sails were finished, ***Mermaid*** was provisioned, fueled, and ready for sea trials. I phoned my friend, Champ Echols in Florida, and invited him to join me as I tried to sink ***Mermaid***. He jumped on an airplane at once, flying to Corpus Christi, Texas for ***Mermaid's*** maiden voyage.

Just before a big storm from the northwest (nor'wester) blew in, we moved out through Aransas Pass into the Gulf of Mexico. I had made up my mind that there would be ***no doubts*** about how seaworthy ***Mermaid*** is. She would either prove herself seaworthy or I would sink her! She had her chance, as we had a sixty-knot wind and a real ride for three of the five days offshore.

The only weaknesses that I found were less than adequate cupboard latches and the absolute necessity to secure the mattresses properly. The lesson about securing the mattresses made a deep impression on me. We were heaved to and rolling a fair bit. The bunks are across from each other amidships. ***Mermaid*** took a big roll. I rolled out of the bunk onto the cabin sole (floor). My mattress tumbled out on top of me. On the back roll, Champ came riding out on his mattress, which landed on my mattress on top of me.

As we sorted this out, I said, *"I hope you weren't hurt!"*

Champ replied, *"It just goes to show that when you live right, a mattress will even take care of you at sea."*

With the sea test complete, I took ***Mermaid*** across the Gulf, staying a bit south in order to keep warmer and to practice the celestial navigation I had learned through a navigation correspondence course. We had a good sail, arriving at Cape Coral, Florida where I secured ***Mermaid*** at the marina.

From 1979 to 1988, I sailed alone, with my family, or with my friends on ***Mermaid*** in the Gulf of Mexico, the Caribbean, and the waters around Florida. She gave us great pleasure and adventure. Now, my mistress was provisioned and ready to take ***"The Big Trip"*** and then ***"The Trip Around the World!"***

THE BIG TRIP

May, 1988: The dream was about to happen! After many years of thinking about sailing around the world, I was about to set sail. I had read about almost every other small boat sailor from our very own Joshua Slocum to Eric and Susan Hiscock. Now, ***Mermaid*** and I were in Titusville, Florida, waiting for my youngest daughter, Kelly, to come aboard to sail across the Atlantic-the start of a sailing adventure that would take me around the North Atlantic and then around the world, and that I would complete in 1993.

Kelly arrived on May 6. It was very fortunate that she was on college break for the summer and wanted to crew across the Atlantic with me. She had always been a good sailor growing up. So, it was no surprise when her summer study plans went out the window at the opportunity for the sailing adventure.

I've got three beautiful daughters, each one a good sailor. Kelly gained everybody's respect early in her sailing career. You can understand why when you learn her well-earned nickname: ***"Irongut."***

May 6, 1988: Kelly and I left Titusville, Florida at 2130 local time (LT) with a northwest wind at twenty knots. The wind gradually shifted to the north. We were sailing close to the wind, heading north of the Bahamas and using the Gulf Stream to push us north northeast.

May 10: We were at 32 degrees north latitude, running east directly toward Bermuda with a light south wind shifting to southwest. At 0700 LT, we caught a dorado, which took a great leap and broke thc hook on our fifty-pound test line.

May 11: The wind dropped to less than five knots from the east. Our position was 32 degrees 17 minutes north, 68 degrees 55 minutes west. Three ships passed us going north and south in the last two days. We sighted two whales about one hundred yards away. They sounded immediately. We had had fog with a half-mile visibility the previous night. By afternoon, the sky was clear with some cumulus clouds starting to appear.

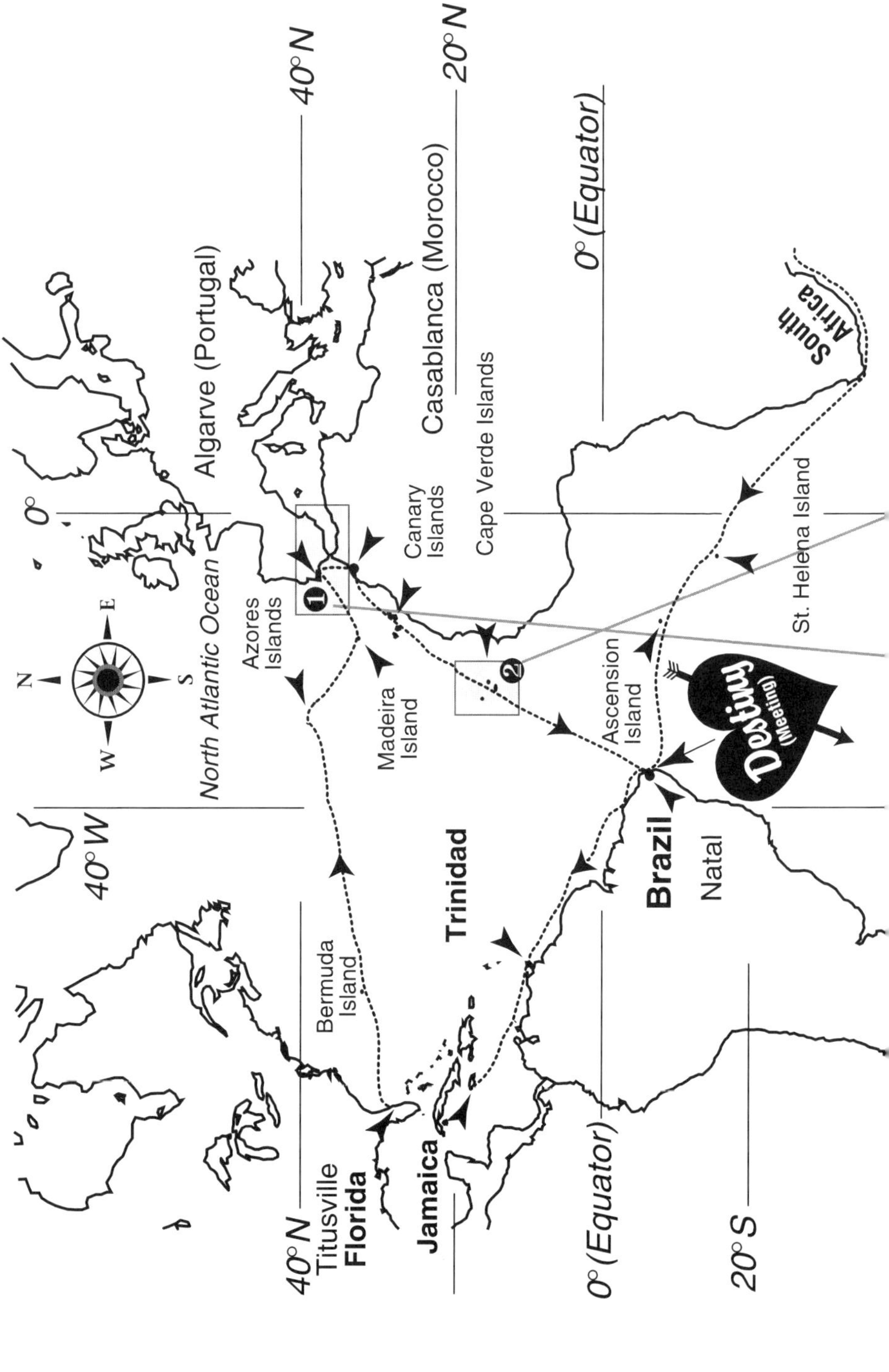

40° N
20° N
0° (Equator)
0°
40° W
40° N
0° (Equator)
20° S
N
S
E
W
North Atlantic Ocean
Algarve (Portugal)
Casablanca (Morocco)
Cape Verde Islands
Canary Islands
Azores Islands
Madeira Island
Cape Verde Islands
St. Helena Island
Ascension Island
South Africa
Destiny
(Meeting)
Brazil
Natal
Trinidad
Bermuda Island
Titusville
Florida
Jamaica
1
2

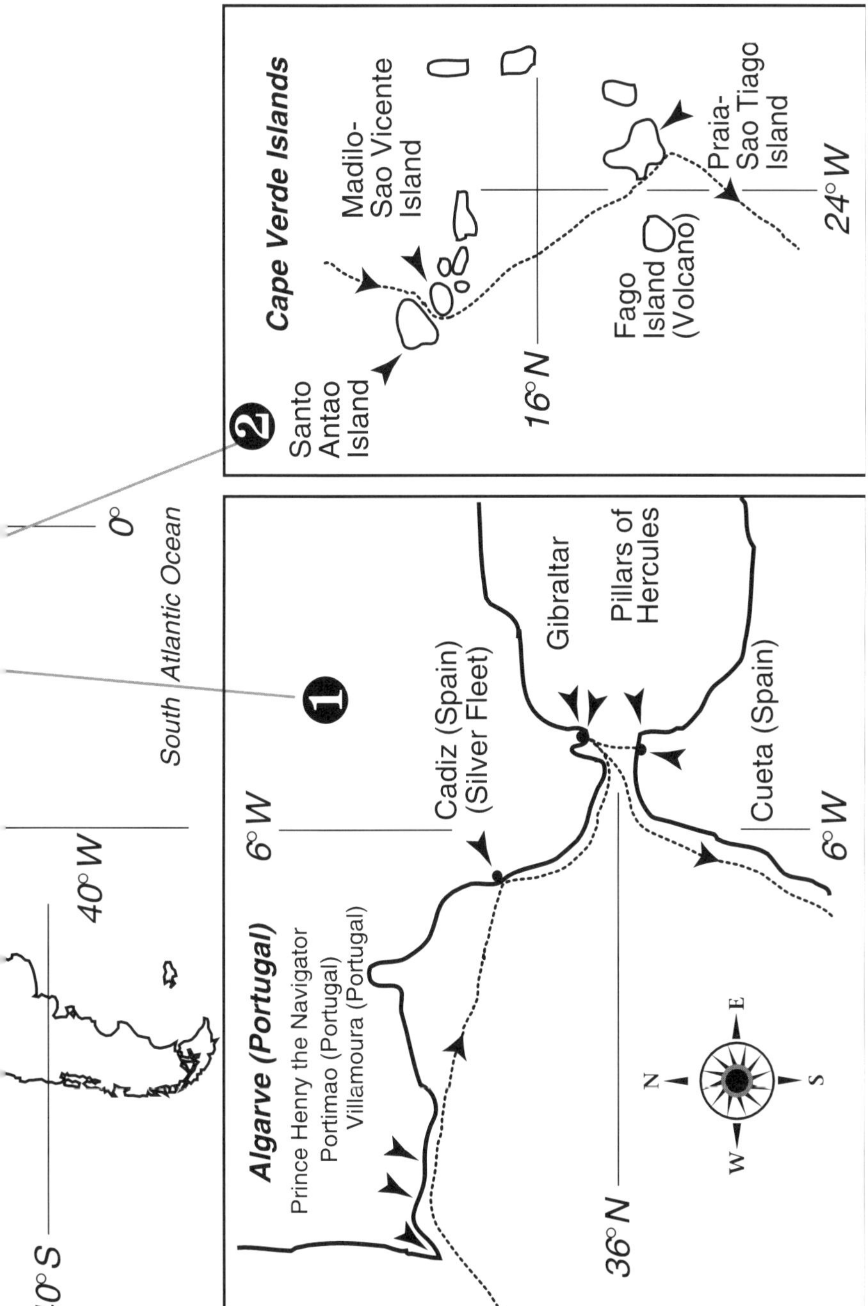
40° S
40° W
0°
South Atlantic Ocean
Cape Verde Islands
Santo Antao Island
Madilo-Sao Vicente Island
Fago Island (Volcano)
Praia-Sao Tiago Island
16° N
24° W
Algarve (Portugal)
Prince Henry the Navigator
Portimao (Portugal)
Villamoura (Portugal)
Cadiz (Spain) (Silver Fleet)
Gibraltar
Pillars of Hercules
Cueta (Spain)
6° W
6° W
36° N
N
E
S
W

MY PARROT

One time I had a parrot aboard
He thought he was lord
He would never let you get bored
Because he was never moored.

Into the rigging he would go
Climbing to the peak with that "BEAK"
And screeching at everybody galore.

One day the hand of fate
Made him lose his gait
And he fell overboard
And nearly got ate.

To his great relief he floated
And soon I had him boated
And we both gloated
And he was grateful for an hour more.

May 14: We motored in a calm with a small ocean swell coming from the east. Our magnetic compass course was corrected for a fourteen degree west variation.

May 15: We arrived on the southwest end of Bermuda and sailed up the coast with an east northeast heading to Saint George Bay. By good fortune, we arrived just as the Jimmy Cornell Atlantic Race for cruising boats (ARC) was leaving. What a beautiful sight! There were spinnakers of every color flying! There must have been more than a hundred boats! Their departure by no means left the Saint George Bay anchorage empty, but it did make it easier to find a place to anchor. Before anchoring, we went to the customs dock and rafted up with the other boats waiting to clear. Clearing in was efficient and, at the time, twenty dollars U.S. per person. Both St. George Bay and Hamilton Harbor are great crossroads for boats going from the United States to Europe and from the eastern Caribbean to the northeast United States and Canada for the summer season. The traffic is reversed for the winter season: from the northeast back to the Caribbean. For the eastbound traveler, it is a particularly good route, as the westerly wind prevails. We were looking for the westerlies. Bermuda is a nice rest stop. But like most eastbound sailors, we were ***anxious*** to get going. The next leg was to be the longest of our eastward Atlantic passage.

May 19: At 1500 LT, we departed Saint George Bay, Bermuda, en route to the town of Horta on the island of Fayal in the Azores. The wind was south southwest at ten to fifteen knots. After referring to the pilot charts for the North Atlantic, we set a course for ***Mermaid*** to run at 063 degrees true to 37 degrees 30 minutes north and 52 degrees 10 minutes west. From there, we planned to run on the 37 degrees 30 minute north latitude to the Azores. Should we encounter calms or head wind, we would work north until the westerlies prevailed.

May 20: We ran with a south wind blowing ten to fifteen knots. The temperature was 70 degrees F. There were stratocumulus clouds with nine-tenths cover and occasional misty rain. Later in the day, the sky cleared.

May 21: The wind shifted to southeast at ten to fifteen knots. Our course was 076 degrees true. Today we sighted three pilot whales and a "square grouper" (a term for a bale of marijuana).

May 22: The wind returned to south to southwest at twenty knots. The sky was overcast with cirrostratus and altostratus clouds. There were also some cumulonimbus (thunderstorm) clouds that were building. I saw the sun twice, passing a small opening in the clouds, and was able to make quick measurements with my sextant for a two-line position. Dolphins were running with us today.

May 24: A cold front came through at 0200 LT with a lot of rain and shifting wind. It was cold and miserable. We dropped the sails and went to bed. The front passed in the late morning and the wind moved back to the south with a clearing sky. Still later, it became overcast again.

May 25: The wind dropped and we motored for fourteen hours. Then the wind returned from south southwest at fifteen to twenty knots. Our position was 36 degrees 05 minutes north and 53 degrees 07 minutes west.

May 26: The wind was southwest at ten knots. The sky was clear. It was 76 degrees F below deck.

May 27: The wind was south southwest at ten to fifteen knots.

May 28: The wind was southwest at fifteen knots. It was sunny with scattered clouds.

May 29: The wind was west southwest at fifteen knots. Our course was 090 degrees true. Our position was 37 degrees 21 minutes north and 44 degrees 38 minutes west. The clouds were high cirrus and cumulus with five tenths of the sky covered. We hit a floating wood platform about four by eight feet. There was no damage to ***Mermaid***.

May 30, 31, June 1, 2, and 3: The weather pattern had little change. Our June 3 position was 38 degrees 05 minutes north and 30 degrees 41 minutes west.

AZORES

June 4, 1988: All the boats entering the Azores, no matter what their eventual destinations, are requested to clear customs at Horta on Fayal Island. Once cleared there, it is mandatory to use their marina by the customs dock. ***Mermaid*** arrived at the customs dock in Horta at 1500 LT, completing the longest leg of our eastbound transatlantic passage. The cost of a berth in the marina for ***Mermaid*** would have been approximately $3.25 U.S. a day, including electricity and water. However, when we arrived, the Atlantic Racing Cruisers (ARC) were still there, filling up the marina. Consequently, we had to pick up a buoy in the harbor. This suited us just fine. An hour later, the dinghy was down and the ***Mermaid*** was set for buoy living.

Our sail to Horta had taken a course a bit south of our planned route because the wind was accommodating. It had been possible to get a celestial position every day in the latitudes we had sailed. I could usually get three sun lines or star shots, but always at least two sun lines at sometime during the day. Kelly and I were happy to stay south for the warmer temperatures. Moreover, if we got blasted by a nor'wester, we hoped it would have moderated by the time it got to us. Indeed, this proved to be the case for the one cold front that did pass us.

While talking to cruisers who arrived in Horta around the same time we did, we learned that several had opted to sail across at the 40 degree north latitude or even further north, in order to take advantage of stronger westerlies. They got blasted with a forty-knot wind in the frontal storm.The very same storm, by the time when it passed ***Mermaid***, had moderated. Nevertheless, it brought cold and heavy rain. Reading my log now, I marvel that it was necessary only to drop our sails, in contrast with the usual storm tactic of hanging a small area of sail, sheeted in, and heading the boat to windward, lashing the tiller over (heaving to). This procedure decreases the movements of the boat, making an easier ride in a storm. Heaving to is also a good tactic to use when waiting to close a shore. For the two of us, the frontal storm with its cold, heavy rain was merely a break for some sleep. I recall the thunder and lightning and the pounding of the rain on ***Mermaid***. It was so nice and warm below, wrapped in my blankets. That pounding rain just made me sleep like a baby. ***The heavy rain calmed the sea.*** Eventually, the fast shifting wind and velocity abated as it was a small, fast moving front.

This Atlantic crossing was the first time that ***Mermaid*** and her crew had made a fifteen day passage. It made me realize how fast time flies at sea. The days flow together and the routine is all that matters. Then there is the freedom-the glorious freedom of the open sea that landlubbers will never experience!

June 7, 1988: We left Horta and sailed to Angra on the island of Terceira, clearing in on June 8. It is required to clear in and out of every port when sailing in Portuguese waters. This is a matter of having the papers stamped that you get at your first port of entry-for us Horta. Angra is a fair harbor. Its yacht density was minimal: two boats in the harbor in contrast to well over one hundred in Horta.

June 11: We sailed to Ponta Delgada on San Miguel Island where we picked up a buoy. This is another good harbor. Ponta Delgada is an industrial harbor and a good place for provisioning as there are many stores. The harbor boasts a floating dock so that yachts can raft together if desired. While we were there, there were fifteen yachts rafted and three on buoys.

The Azores are high, weathered mountains with a great deal of cultivation. There are stone fences everywhere to attest to the difficulty in clearing the land. All the islands are clean and neat. The people are friendly and courteous. The exchange rate was 140 escudos for $1.00 U.S. Diesel fuel was 58.5 escudos per imperial gallon (five quarts). An imperial gallon of wine was 650 escudos and cheese was 750 escudos per kilo (2.2 lbs). If you love to eat cheese, bread, and wine, you will enjoy the Azores tremendously at a very reasonable cost.

Sailing through the Azores, we had a north northeast wind at fifteen to twenty knots with a five-tenths cloud cover and occasional rain showers.

MADEIRA

June 13, 1988: At 1600 LT, Mermaid departed from San Miguel Island en route to Funchal, Madiera. Since the wind was right for passage, it seemed that we should take advantage of it. ***Mermaid*** took up a 124 degree true heading with a north northeast to northeast wind of fifteen knots, steady. The sky was a five-tenths broken condition with scattered showers.

June 14: The sky was clearing and the temperature warming. The wind was northeast at ten to fifteen knots. The cabin temperature was 72 degrees F.

June 15, 16, and 17: We had a northeast wind blowing ten to fifteen knots. There were scattered clouds and it was nice sailing. We sighted a sea turtle one day. At 1900 LT on the 17th, we sighted the west end of Madeira which was about twelve miles distant.

June 18: We sailed down the south coast of Madeira and anchored east of the marina breakwater. We had reasonable protection from the long breakwater to the west and south of us. The bay also has protection from the east because of its natural indentation. Clearance in was easy and convenient. The marina charged 1600 escudos per day. However, the exchange rate had changed from the Azores. It was 135 escudos to the dollar here because it is a tourist area.

Mermaid was anchored near a very narrow-hulled catamaran with no mast which had become a nesting area for seagulls. The boat had been anchored there a couple years. Its mast was lying on the seawall to the southwest. We learned it had been a French racing catamaran which had pitch-poled south of Madeira in a race, and had been towed to this spot. Now it just sits and deteriorates at anchor. You would cry if you saw six of the biggest sheet winches money can buy on that boat in total neglect and probably no longer usable. Don't worry! I cried enough for all of us!

Indeed, Funchal seems to be a dumping ground for good sea boats. At the marina, there were a number of yachts whose owners the marina had no idea how to contact. The marina hadn't been paid in a couple of years. These boats also just sit there deteriorating.

Another boat had been impounded by the police. The skipper had apparently sailed in with a great deal of money aboard. He was regarded as suspicious. The police checked with Interpol and found that he was wanted in another country. So he was arrested, and that boat just sits there as well.

On our second day in Funchal, an old poorly maintained Baltic schooner sailed in and tied up at the marina. With a pretty grubby lot for a crew and a couple of kids aboard, I wondered, "How will they pay for their marina berth?" While in town that day, I found out. They sent the kids into town with a couple of cans with a slot in the top like a piggy bank for dropping in money. On the can was a sign which said, *"Please help! It is better to beg than to steal!"*

Madeira is the most beautiful island I cruised to in the North Atlantic. It looks very much like a tropical island. The natives grow bananas and papaya on the south coast and vegetables on the north coast. There are fabulous hiking trails through the mountains and the greenery is wonderful. One hiking trail that stands out in my memory was on a ridge of volcanic mountains with a one thousand-foot drop-off on both sides, and with only a three-foot wide walkway on top. Fortunately, it had a rail that was cemented in to hang onto.

PORTUGAL AND SPAIN

June 22, 1988: The wind was still holding to the north northeast. At 1600 LT, we departed Funchal. We sailed past Porto Santo Island that night with the wind moving more north at eight to ten knots.

June 23, 24: We were sailing at 060 degrees true. The wind was north at ten knots and the sky was overcast.

June 25, 26: The sky had cleared and the wind was north at ten knots. On the 26th, our position was 36 degrees 10 minutes north and 10 degrees 42 minutes west. There is certainly no mistaking when you are nearing Portugal. The line of shipping going to and from the Strait of Gibraltar is like a turnpike on the ocean. Even though the shipping is heavy, once in the strait it is quite easy to avoid it by sailing close to the coast. There, the fishing vessels, their fishing net buoys, and other small crafts are a person's chief worries.

Usually, the wind near the strait is calm in the morning. When you pull the anchor, it may seem that a light air condition will prevail all day and that you can tow your dinghy. However, by afternoon, a wind of twenty-five to thirty knots or better is very likely to be blowing at you or behind you. Whether from east or west, this wind should pose no problems-unless you have a dinghy bouncing behind you, filling with water because of the short chop one gets with the wind and strong currents.

June 27: We arrived at Portimao, Portugal, sailing by Prince Henry the Navigator's Monastery, located at the southwest tip of Portugal in Segres. Without a doubt, Portimao was my favorite stop on the south Portugal coast. The harbor consists of two man-made breakwaters built outside a river mouth. On entering between them, we turned east and anchored behind them in ten feet of water at low tide.

What a beautiful anchorage! There are two hundred-foot cliffs to the east with very colorful rocks and caves. To the north, there is a six hundred-year-old monastery. Beyond that, along the river, lies the city of Portimao, about one mile from our anchorage. It is a reasonably quiet anchorage with the wind usually blowing from the east or west.

To the west lie the famous beaches of the Algarve. These stand out in my memory as a most unique experience. I suspect this would be true for most of the males of our species on the planet. Picture thousands of lovely women parading around and sunbathing with their bikini tops off! That is the Algarve. It's a presentation of the beautiful human being called woman. Your eyes can take in the variety and wonder of woman and retain the mystery of not seeing all.

Departing Portimao on July 1, 1988, we sailed to the resort of Villamora, arriving the same day. Welcome back to the ***Concrete Jungle***! From Horta to Portimao, I had used the same clearance papers, getting them stamped at each new port. This didn't work at Villamora. We had to stand off the customs dock and wait for room to tie up. When we were finally secured at the dock, we had to go through another full clearance procedure and pay for entry all over again.

After clearing in, ***Mermaid*** was assigned a berth. It was late afternoon with a strong west wind and a flooding tide. Our berth was down a finger to the east. When we turned down the entrance to our berth, a strong wind and a two-knot current were behind us. Not fun! There were millions of dollars worth of boats on both sides, a current and wind behind us, and a jagged rock seawall ahead of us. We had a small two-bladed propeller which we used for long ocean passages to reduce prop drag. Unfortunately, it didn't have enough torque to twist ***Mermaid*** around in that confined space with so much wind and current on her broadside. Consequently, we missed our berth and were on a fast clip down the channel toward the jagged rock seawall ahead! We were able to turn the boat sideways to the wind, but couldn't keep the swing going in that confined space, even though I was turning to the ***right with a right-hand prop,*** allowing the prop torque to assist me. I was ready to drop anchor right in the center of that channel in order to taut up, and get the bow around to stop our progression toward that dead-end rock seawall. At that moment, a fellow yachtsman came topside, a couple of boats down the channel from us, and saw our plight. I asked him to secure our bow so that we could complete our turn. He complied and the ***Mermaid*** turned to the current and the wind. Thankfully, the emergency was over. We headed into the wind and current, and had no further problems getting into our berth.

While in Villamora, we took in a bull fight at the bull ring, one mile away. The exchange rate was 145 escudos to the U.S. dollar. The marina fee was 1480 escudos per day. We also checked out the cost of a hotel room: $140.00 U.S. a day.

July 6, 1988: We sailed from Villamora and arrived in Ayamonte, Spain on the same day. Ayamonte has easy clearance at the ferry dock. The anchorage is in the Guadiana River to the west of the town. It is a very rolling anchorage in the afternoon with the strong sea breeze. There is a small lagoon south of town, but I preferred the river for anchoring.

Ayamonte is a good place to provision. I found ***all the prices in Spain*** to be more expensive than in the United States. The traveler should plan on paying more for everything than he may be used to, especially when just arriving from stateside. In Ayamonte, at least I could get almost everything I needed.

July 7: We departed from Ayamonte in a flat calm at 0600 LT and motored until the wind picked up. We arrived at Cadiz, Spain at 2000 LT with the wind west southwest at twenty-five knots and the waves from the southwest. We anchored south of the large boat dry docks on the east side of the city. This anchorage proved to be very good.

Cadiz is an old city. The older part is around five hundred years old while the newer part is about two hundred years old. The churches seem to hold most of the history and existing artifacts. The artifact or art buff should head for the churches. We went to a museum and saw some damaged Roman statues and a Phoenician coffin.

It was getting close to college time. Kelly had to return to the United States. We took ***Mermaid*** across the bay to Puerto Sherry, a new and very nice marina. At the time, the cost was 950 pesetas per day in-season and 500 pesetas per day off-season. The busy season is from June 1 to October 31. The money exchange was 120 pesetas for $1.00 U.S. We left the boat at Puerto Sherry and took a train from Santa Maria to Madrid. I wish I could say it was a pleasant ride. It wasn't! Not realizing that there are separate cars for smokers and non-smokers, we settled into a smoking car. Neither of us had enough sense to go through the train to find more acceptable accommodations. So, we sat there enduring one of the greatest chain-smoking societies I have ever encountered.

In Madrid, I purchased an airline ticket for Kelly and I bid my good sailing buddy good-bye. Standing in that ticket line, I suddenly realized just how much a fifteen-day passage at sea to any destination is to be preferred over standing in airport lines. What a warm feeling it was to realize that I'd soon be back on board ***Mermaid***, enjoying the freedom of the sea.

Returning to Puerto Sherry late one evening in August, I had a ***real shock!*** I didn't find ***Mermaid*** where I had left her. I searched through the marina for thirty minutes. I checked with the night watchman, but to no avail. I came to the agonizing conclusion that ***Mermaid*** had been stolen. In desperation, I decided to make one more thorough search, walking every inch of every pier in the marina. At last, I sighted her at the far end of a pier where there were a few yachts and many empty berths. The lighting in that area was poor. That was why I had missed her the first time through. Presumably, when no one was aboard ***Mermaid*** for some time, the marina people took the liberty of moving her from where I had been instructed to tie her, to this less busy area in order to make room for transient boats at the main berths. What a relief to find my ***Mermaid***! The next morning, she and I were underway once more for Gibraltar and then the Atlantic.

August 13, 1988: The trip from Puerto Sherry to Gilbraltar was mostly motoring with foggy conditions. There was sufficient visibility during the night to navigate by the beacons onshore. In the morning, there was fog with visibility from one-half to two miles. A light west wind came up and moved the fog out. Thirty minutes later, a light east wind blew the fog back over me. Later, an east wind blew it out and then the east wind brought more fog. Believe me when I say it was really tough to read a weather pattern out there!

August 14: At 1600 LT, I tied to the British Customs Dock at Gibraltar and cleared in. Then I moved to an anchorage north of the west end of the airport runway. From this anchorage, I saw the Rock of Gibraltar, which has a lot of history surrounding it. The openings are visible in the side of the rock where the British accidentally broke through while digging an inside tunnel in order to get cannon to the top. Once the hole had been broken, they realized what a good idea it was to mount the guns at different openings going up the tunnel to the top. That gave them gun ports overlooking Spain, which enabled them to prevent invaders from the land from taking the rock. Also to be seen from my anchorage, was an old Moorish fortification with its bathhouses for cleanliness.

Gibraltar is a great place for would-be sailors who want to crew to catch a lift to the Caribbean. While there, many yachtsmen look for crew to help them take the trade wind route to the West Indies. I was told that in October quite a lot of potential crewmen flood into Gibraltar, looking for opportunities to sail west. While I was there, unfortunately, the pickings were so slim that I opted to sail alone.

During my stay in Gibraltar, it was necessary to buy provisions and propane for the next passage ahead. At that time, one British pound exchanged for $1.73 U.S. A fellow yachtsman, who sails that area, advised me to sail to Ceuta, Spain. Ceuta is a Spanish possession across the strait on the north coast of Morocco. He said there would be no problems in filling a U.S.

propane bottle and that provisions would be less costly. Both of these statements proved to be true. It is a short sail. Provisions are easy to get, as well as water and propane. There is a good seawall to tie to. However, since Ceuta is a petroleum port, I expected a dirty waterline and fenders. To counter this, while there, I purchased CIF in Spanish (JIFF in English). This cleanser cut the oil off, fast and easy, and was recommended by a yachtsman who lives on his boat there. He must have had a lot of experience cleaning oil off his boat in Ceuta.

September 3, 1988: ***Mermaid*** departed Gibraltar at 0700 LT. The wind was light and I was motoring. The Straits of Gibraltar can be dangerous due to the heavy shipping. This brings to mind a story I heard two years later while at the Panama Canal regarding a remarkable experience I heard first-hand from two world cruisers, who were just beginning their last leg across the Pacific from the canal to Hawaii.

I met Dick and his wife Bonnie when helping to line-handle their boat through the canal. The true story of their experience in the Straits of Gibraltar sent chills up and down my spine, as it underlines the dangers of sailing with heavy shipping around the world.

It was a beautiful, clear night. The wind had dropped to nothing. With sails up, Dick and Bonnie were just drifting along in the strait between Gibraltar and the town of Algeciras on the Spanish coast, which they could see very well. At about 0200 LT, a freighter came out of the harbor of Algeciras and turned offshore, putting Dick and Bonnie's boat right on its heading! As the ship approached, it became apparent that no one aboard the freighter saw the smaller vessel. Dick attempted to radio them, but did not get a response. He immediately went below to start the engine in order to motor out of the freighter's way. About thirty seconds elapsed when the engine quit! So, there they were, sails up, with no wind, no engine, and no contact with the freighter bearing down on them at steerage speed. Their boat was just under forty feet in length with a fin keel. The large ship never saw it! Instead, the freighter hit the small boat broadside. The bow flow of water lifted the small sailing vessel over the freighter's bulbous protrusion, and wedged it there with the fin forward and the skeg and rudder aft, laying a bit over since the top shroud was resting against the rail at the top of the freighter's bow. Dick thought, *"What do I do now? Should I climb the mast steps and get onto the freighter's bow?"* A few seconds later, his boat washed over the bulb and drifted down the side of the freighter with its top shroud rubbing the freighter's side the full length. Dick and Bonnie searched their boat for holes desperately. *"Is water coming in?"* they worried. There were small broken pieces of unknown origin scattered all over the deck. *"Were they chunks of fiberglass from damage to their boat?"*

After thoroughly going over their vessel, to their absolute astonishment, they found it wasn't taking water! More investigation revealed that the material on the deck was paint scrapings resulting from the top shroud rubbing on the freighter's side as it steamed past them. The scrapings were from the freighter, not from their boat. Everything had happened so fast that it seemed unreal. But they couldn't have imagined it since the paint scrapings were on their deck. All was quiet and peaceful once more. In the morning, they got a tow into Algeciras. There, they had the boat checked over to determine what repairs had to be made. Miraculously, the only repair needed was to their bent rudder. Fortunately, their fin-keel boat design had a protected propeller between the skeg and rudder. This prevented damage to the shaft and the prop.

September 3,1988: After departing Gibraltar in the morning, I witnessed a dramatic demonstration of just how strong the currents coming into the Straits of Gibraltar from the Atlantic really are. A Swedish vessel, about sixty feet long, but with no engine, had sailed out of the same port the day before, headed west with an easterly breeze. Now, a day later, I easily motored past her, not long after I had left port. She had started with a brisk, afternoon breeze. It dropped in the night. She drifted back east and was just getting started again when I passed her.

Sailing these waters brings great respect for all the skippers who sailed them throughout history. Many great sea battles were fought here among the English, French, Spanish, and other navies. How did they wage those battles with such variable wind? It's easy to imagine the great fleets waiting to wage war while they drifted in the current until the afternoon sea breeze came up, or to see them getting blasted with strong wind from any direction, having to beat to windward against the current and making very little progress. Even more remarkable is that they sailed in winter with cold freezing rain, fog, nor'westers, and nor'easters while beating against the strong wind and currents. They had to be miserable, but they were surely tough.

CASABLANCA, MOROCCO

September 4, 1988: Moving out of the Straits of Gibraltar into the Atlantic, I was happy to have an engine for the passage to Casablanca. There was a variable wind condition, going from zero to thirty knots and back, as the day wore on. The sea was choppy without any predominant pattern to it. As I progressed further south, there was less wind and more fog. The day I closed Casablanca, I was fortunate to see the sun for a few minutes around 0700 LT before fog socked in again. This gave me a sun line, one line for calculating position. I also had a depth sounding with a very poor angle of intersect for a second line. With this two-line position, I closed Casablanca.

With the dense fog, I chose not to close direct to Casablanca for two reasons. First, a fair amount of shipping comes and goes from that port. Second, the availability of only two lines for taking a position, with a possible five-mile error, could have had me coming in south of the port in the fog. I plotted a course to the ten-fathom curve, eight miles north of the channel buoy. Fortunately, the channel buoy sits directly on the ten-fathom curve. Consequently, it was just a matter of sounding to the ten-fathom curve and moving south for about an hour or so after getting to the ten-fathom curve, depending on the accuracy of my calculation of position. It worked out beautifully. I was able to stay inside all of the shipping, ***I think***.

September 5, 1988: When I sighted the buoy, I took a short run to the breakwater and entered the harbor of Casablanca. Had my calculations not worked out, it would have been simple to throw the anchor and wait for an opportunity to recalculate my position. As I entered the Casablanca harbor, I was met by a friendly police boat and directed to the marina where they boarded the boat to begin clearing me in. The marina, or yacht club, is in the inner harbor. Mooring is to a buoy, fore and aft, and rafted to other boats. A dinghy is needed for shore access.

The cost of moorage was 70 durum per week, including electricity and water. A long electrical pigtail is required to get to the outlet. The exchange rate was 8.33 durum for $1.00 U.S. Clearance was involved, but it was easy with a bit of walking.

Casablanca was a new experience and a cultural shock for me. In the Casbah, the old part of town, I felt that I had just joined Ali Baba and his band of forty thieves in a movie set in medieval times.There are narrow streets and walkways darkened by two- and three-story buildings. Many of the women are veiled and wear black robes. The men wear turbans. There are vendors with little stands everywhere. Fragrances of spices and fruits fill the air. The fruit and vegetable market was the best I had seen since leaving the states. You name it and you can find it! As I shopped, I was walking shoulder to shoulder with the natives. Most certainly, bargaining is the normal way to purchase items. It is best to have small bills so you can bargain up and pay the exact amount. Don't expect change. Should you pay too much and expect change, the vendor will start new bargaining rather than give you change. Of course, some merchants will give change just as we do, but this is an exception.

I found the natives friendly and interesting. As I walked through the market, a young man stepped in stride with me and spoke English. We struck up a conversation as he offered a guided tour of the area. I have found that most visitors reject this approach and try to shoo the person away. This can be a mistake. Many times this is an opportunity to meet some local natives.

One has to ask, *"What does a person visit another country for?"*

Meeting the noncommercial natives can be interesting and unique. This fellow showed me around and carried a fossil stone I had purchased. Of course, I knew he hoped to make some money and I told him what I would pay before the tour. With this understanding, we had a good visit as I shopped. Most of the vendors knew him and with my guide as interpreter, they took the opportunity to talk to me. They were pleased to see a friendly tourist that they could communicate with.

"How do you like my country?" asked one man.

Another man told me proudly, *"My son lives in New York."*

I told him I had been to New York and it was nice. This made him happy.

After I was finished shopping and had returned to the harbor, I thanked my guide for the interesting tour. He also thanked me and told me to never change. He sincerely appreciated my ***kindness and friendliness.***

While at the yacht club in Casablanca, I was tied to a British sailboat. The owner had hired a local fellow to do some fiberglass work. After I became aquainted with him, he asked if he could sail to Las Palmas in the Canaries with me and bring his girlfriend. Since I was sailing alone and liked him, I agreed. I took them on as crew for that leg.

LAS PALMAS, CANARIES

September 9,1988 : The Mermaid departed Casablanca at 1700 LT in light air and a small swell from the northwest. Our course was 270 degrees true. A school of tuna ran with us. We put over a shiny spoon lure. It was immediately taken by an eight-kilo tuna, which we ate for dinner, breakfast, and lunch the next day.

On our way to Las Palmas, Canary Islands, there was plenty of time for conversation. My crew were a French Moroccan and his Dutch Moroccan girlfriend. He was traveling on a French passport and she was traveling on a Dutch passport. Since they told me they had lived in Morocco all their lives, I asked why they weren't carrying Moroccan passports.They explained that it's very difficult to get a Moroccan passport, especially for a woman. One could wait as long as ten years and then still have to pay a bribe to a government official.

September 11: The wind was north at fifteen to twenty knots. The sky was broken to overcast.

September 12: The sky was clearing. Our course was 213 degrees true and our position was 30 degrees 55 minutes north and 13 degrees 21 minutes west.

September 13: The wind was north northeast at four knots. We motor-sailed, steering 200 degrees true in haze and limited visibility.

September 14: We arrived at Las Palmas in dense haze with three miles visibility or less. It was possible to get a sun line position. This plotted us closing Grand Canary Island. We were close to the island, but we could not see it. At sunset, the northeast navigational light blasted through the dense haze about two miles from us. We closed past the light and motored to Las Palmas, four miles south. It was well lit. Finding the yacht club wasn't difficult.

I had heard that Las Palmas had dirty, oily water, but found the water quite clean while I was there. It is a totally manmade port with breakwaters which afford good protection. We had a good anchorage by the yacht club with access to water and a garbage barrel. It is an easy walk to town and a good provisioning stop.

A number of yachts were in the port. One, from South Africa, had been demasted off the Cape Verde Islands. Her skipper had motored to Grand Canary Island and was waiting for a new mast to be shipped from South Africa. Another American vessel arrived from San Francisco, via the Pacific and Indian Oceans, and the Red and Mediterranean Seas, down to Las Palmas. Her skipper was waiting for a new main sail, jib, and transmission. I also met a couple from Canada. They had taken a year off to sail to Europe. Now they were returning to the Caribbean for the winter before they headed back to Montreal in June. ***Pampero II,*** an Australian boat, was circumnavigating by way of the Red Sea. I was to meet up with them later in Salinas, Ecuador.

Las Palmas is another good place for providing sailing enthusiasts the opportunity to crew aboard yachts headed for the Caribbean. There is a bulletin board where would-be sailors can post notes soliciting rides to the Caribbean in crewing positions. It was the time of year for many yachts to come in port as part of the traditional migration across the warm northeast trade wind to the lovely Caribbean. Many others were coming in to sail in the November ARC sponsored cruising race. It was rumored that about two hundred boats were expected to participate. Most ccrtainly, the anchorage would be filling up very soon.

CAPE VERDE ISLANDS

September 24, 1988: I departed Las Palmas in order to get clear of the upcoming big race group there, and single-handed to the Cape Verde Islands. When I left Las Palmas at 1430 LT, the wind was north northeast at fifteen knots. In the evening, the wind dropped and the motoring began.

September 25: While I was motoring on a flat sea, a shark swam by with its fin protruding above the surface. It was two meters long. A small tuna escorted ***Mermaid*** off the starboard bow for an hour or more. The water gradually became clear and deep blue. The sky had a scattered condition with cumulus clouds from the southeast.

September 26: The wind was light and variable, and a hazy condition gave way to a clear horizon. That evening, there was a very bright, green flash at sunset, almost like a camera flash-bulb going off. Later, the wind picked up out of the north north-east, blowing at twenty knots.

THE GREEN FLASH

To see a green flash,

You must have blue water, which is deep water,

A clear horizon,

And a red setting sun.

You will see the flash just as the TOP of the sun's sphere touches the horizon as it sets.

September 27: The wind was north northeast at twenty knots. The waves were five to eight feet. My course was 225 degrees true and there was a thin cirrus overcast.

September 28: The wind was north northeast at twenty-five knots and the waves were five to eight feet with a ten-foot ocean swell. The sea condition was rolling with cross seas. My position was 22 degrees 51 minutes north and 20 degrees 31 minutes west.

September 29: The wind pattern stayed the same except for a lovely warming. This differs from the more northerly latitudes where the wind can be warm, but always has a bit of a chill in it. The boat temperature was 80 degrees F.

September 30: The wind was from the northeast at ten knots and less. The clouds were stratocumulus in a broken cloud cover and the cabin temperature was 82 degrees F. I sighted a ship going north about two miles west of me.

October 1: The wind dropped to five knots from the northeast. My position was 19 degrees 22 minutes north and 23 degrees 55 minutes west.

October 2: The sky had scattered cumulus, and it was bright and sunny. ***Mermaid*** arrived at Mindelo, Sao Vicente, Cape Verde Islands at 1500 LT after standing off the early morning hours waiting for daylight to close up shore. The islands were covered with haze. I sighted them at less than five miles. I found that I could be very near these islands in the North Atlantic without seeing them. This was a good test of my celestial navigation skills. Closing the island, I was struck by the desolate, unproductive landscape. It is volcanic. One hardly sees a blade of grass or a tree. There is only rock and sand.

Clearance into Mindelo was straight-forward. I flew the quarantine flag. Immigration came to the boat. The authorities held my passport until I cleared out. They also warned me to always have someone aboard to prevent theft. I hired one of the men onshore who was recommended to me at 700 escudos for twelve hours. You could also pay half that for six hours. The exchange rate was 73 escudos to $1.00 U.S. I locked the boat before leaving it. The guard stayed in the cockpit and never had access below.

The harbor of Mindelo affords good protection. However, every day the land heats up because of the barren terrain. The difference in temperature between land and sea reinforces the trade wind. This can blow up a thirty- to forty-knot wind, which can raise a fair chop in the harbor one hundred meters offshore. Indeed, I found Cape Verde to be a very windy place to sail. This impression was reinforced by seeing yet another demasted boat in dry dock at Mindelo.

I enjoyed meeting the natives of Mindelo. I found them friendly and helpful. Mindelo turned out to be a waiting area and jumping off point for many West Africans who had managed to get that far in hopes of catching a ship or a yacht to the West Indies. I was solicited by many of them who were trying to catch a lift west. However, I found myself unwilling to take the risk. I did not want to get bogged down in immigration problems on clearing into another country. All countries require that you have enough money to stay even a short time. None of these folks had much money to sustain themselves. Most of them seemed to be nice people who were trying for a better life with everything stacked against them.

While in Mindelo, I met a German named Wolfgang who had his boat onshore. He was happy to be working on it because he had almost lost his boat. ***While in the Canaries,*** he had wanted to take on a crewman. He met a fellow who seemed to fit his requirements and took him aboard. A few weeks later, Wolfgang had to fly back to Germany for a few days. His crewman was to watch the boat. When he returned, his boat was gone and had been for two days. He hired an airplane. With the air search, he spotted his boat on a course to the Cape Verde Islands. Upon his return to the Canaries, he notified the Cape Verde Police and Immigration to apprehend this fellow and hold the boat, since it was his and the fellow had stolen it. When the boat arrived, the police arrested the thief and Wolfgang got his boat back. Now, the thief was on the hot seat at the police station. He faced a very unpleasant jail sentence. Of course, they would go easier on him if he did some talking. They learned that this was the ***fifth*** boat he had stolen! He was smuggling them to Bahia Salvador, Brazil where they were illegally documented and sold.

October 8,1988: At 0530 LT, ***Mermaid*** departed Mindelo with wind gusting to thirty knots out of the northeast. I single-handed down the coast with the wind holding at twenty to thirty knots. I was en route to Praia, Sao Tiago Island, Cape Verde to pick up a visa for Brazil.

October 9: While sailing down the coast of Sao Tiago, it was obvious that, unlike Sao Vicente, this island had some vegetation. As I rounded the south end at 1530 LT, the wind dropped to calm. About an hour later, the wind blasted ***Mermaid*** on the bow out of the southeast at thirty knots as I was on course to close Praia. Beating to windward is no fun! Since I was only twenty miles from Praia, I beat. Inspecting the chart, I saw that Praia is an open bay to the southeast and the thirty-knot wind was blowing right into it. Consequently, the anchorage would be rough and unprotected with a lee shore, a condition I did not desire! I had a decision to make: I could stand off Praia until conditions moderated in order to pick up a visa for Brazil, or I could turn directly to Brazil with no visa. I was longing for the peace of the open sea. I wanted to get away from the island and its reinforced wind. I also wanted to close up some of the 1800 miles between my current position and Brazil. It took only a moment to come to a decision. I would take my chances with no visa. After all, if Brazil should give me visa problems, I could sail out of there, too! What a relief it was to put that strong wind on my beam and make some miles toward Brazil.

CUPID'S ARROW

I sailed to the land of the sand
On a close reach with a single-hand
And across the trades I sailed
Planning for my arrival on land.

Clearing in was a bit thin
But with discipline I did win
And stayed in this lovely land
By negotiation with the man.

Off to the market I went
To provision and stay fit
But little did I know
Cupid's arrow would hit.

She walked up behind me
And as I turned and saw that smile
I had the energy to run many miles
It started from there and before I knew it
I had a beautiful gal to sail the miles.

SINGLE-HANDING TO BRAZIL

My pilot charts indicated that, in order to cross the equator while avoiding the doldrums, it's wise to stay around 25 degrees west longitude. It was interesting to see that the heading to get to Brazil from where I was is much more southerly than I supposed. Before actually plotting my course, I had envisioned Brazil to be west of Africa-as it is. However, because of the bulges of Africa and Brazil, it's necessary to sail south to southwest. (Obviously, one reason to go sailing is to learn geography better!)

I made yet another curious discovery. As a sailor of the Caribbean, I had always associated hurricane season with October. As all good Caribbean sailors know, the lows that eventually develop into hurricanes as they cross the Atlantic originate off the Gambian coast. However, when sailing off the coast of West Africa at that very same time of year, those very same lows simply provide good wind to assist the sailor across the equator to get to that southeast trade wind. Once you get to the southeast trade wind and sail with it all the way across to Brazil, you'll most likely find yourself with a wind forward of the beam and sailing close to the wind.

As I left the Cape Verde Islands, there was fine sand on the deck. This condition existed most of the way along the west African coast and far out to sea en route to Brazil. Rarely did I see a red sunset while sailing off Africa, something I like to see with its promise of a fine day tomorrow. Rather, there was always a hazy yellow sunset. Yet the days were fine.

October 10, 1988: The wind was northeast at fifteen to twenty knots.

October 11: My position was 12 degrees 32 minutes north and 24 degrees 32 minutes west. The wind was fifteen knots. There was some heat lightning ahead. The evening was clear and the stars were beautiful!

October 12: The wind was northeast at ten knots and the barometer was dropping slightly. The cloud cover was six tenths with cumulus. My course was 180 degrees true.

October 13: I motored in a light wind with a light sprinkle from stratocumulus clouds. My position was 09 degrees 13 minutes north and 24 degrees 12 minutes west. The wind speed was variable from the north northwest at five knots.

October 14: The wind was variable east to southeast at seven to fifteen knots with gusts in the rain squalls. There were many squalls.

October 15: There was a light southeast breeze and I motor-sailed with a small southeast swell. My position was 06 degrees 39 minutes north and 25 degrees 03 minutes west with rain squalls to twenty knots.

October 16: It was good sailing with the wind south southeast at eight to ten knots. My position was 05 degrees 04 minutes north and 26 degrees 26 minutes west.

October 17: The wind was variable and light, mostly from south to south southeast. It rained all day and I motor-sailed on a 205 degree true course.

October 18: This morning, I took a star shot using Regulus, Canopus, Pollux, and also the planets Jupiter and Venus. My position was 04 degrees 11 minutes north and 27 degrees 18 minutes west. My course was 217 degrees true. The wind was south southeast at fifteen knots and the waves were five to eight feet. ***Mermaid's*** sails were set for a no stress easy ride and I was rocking my way to Brazil on a close reach.

I wash dishes in a bucket, topside, which is usually filled with water. As I was moving around today, I momentarily lost my balance. On catching my balance, my foot stepped into my dishwater bucket, which was fortunately empty of dishes.

October 20: I was sailing with a beautiful, blue sky and sparkling seas. The wind was south southeast at ten knots. My position was 02 degrees 10 minutes north and 29 degrees 24 minutes west. There were a number of birds around today, as well as many schools of flying fish.

October 21: Today with rain squalls and gusting wind, it was necessary to adjust the sails up and down occasionally. I sailed a close reach to windward against an eight-foot wave.

October 22: The wind was southeast at fifteen to twenty knots with a five- to seven-foot wave and a ten-foot ocean swell, all south to south southeast. ***Mermaid*** had been tracking about a twenty-degree side slip, beating to those waves to windward. My course was 211 degrees true and my position was 01 degree 02 minutes south and 31 degrees 31 minutes west.

October 23: I had southeast wind at fifteen to twenty knots on a course of 215 degrees true. The variation here was 20 degrees west.

October 24, 25, 26: The wind was southeast at fifteen to twenty knots. It was great trade wind sailing!

NATAL: MEETING MY DESTINY

When I left Mindelo, I hadn't yet decided just which port in Brazil I would head toward. As a matter of principle, when I cruise I don't set plans in cement. Nor do I ever obligate myself to make contact with anyone at a specific time. My philosophy is that you will hear from me when you hear from me! Obligating yourself to contact someone at a specific time or place puts you on a ***schedule.*** What did you go sailing for in the first place? Moreover, when sailing, at the mercy of the vagaries of the sea, it's tough to know where you'll be at any given time. More often than not, you can't make contact as promised. This pushes everybody's distress buttons. So when I sail, it's footloose and fancy free! Let life take it's own course.

October 25, 1988: I arrived off Natal, Brazil during the night, and stood off overnight. I closed the harbor in the morning of the 26th and anchored at the yacht club. The yacht club was once the officers club when the United States was ferrying war planes to Africa during World War II. It was no mistake to come here! I could see the beautiful city which stands along the shore. The sand beaches are unsurpassed.

When I arrived, there were a few boats anchored off the yacht club. Two were demasted: a French boat and a German boat. An English fellow was also anchored there. I chatted with him to get information on clearance procedure and I mentioned to him that I didn't have a visa. I told him that if necessary, I would fly out of the country to get one if I could leave my boat anchored in Natal. My English friend spoke some Portuguese and offered to help me explain why I had no visa. My clearance papers were from Mindelo to Praia. At least they would prove that I had come from the Cape Verde Islands.

A couple of hours later, the policia federal arrived. They came to the yacht club. When they opened the passport and found no visa, they gave me forty-eight hours and no negotiation. ***Forty-eight hours and out!*** Fine! No big problem for me. I'd only been at sea for eighteen days. ***Have boat, can travel.***

I went about my business by getting a few provisions and loading diesel. That evening, there was a get together at the yacht club. I met the other yachtsmen. There was Alan (the English fellow who had tried to help me) with Judy; another English couple, Eric and Rosilyn on ***Wiggy***; Jock, a Swiss fellow; Denny, a French fellow; and Peter, a German fellow. Jock and Denny were both single-handers. Denny and Peter had both lost their masts in crossing. I also met Zeca, his wife Lucia, and Roberto, local folks who spoke good English. The conversation centered around my forty-eight hours and what to do about it. During the conversation, Paulo, a friend of Roberto's who was listening in, mentioned that his wife worked with the wife of one of the policia federal. He would ask her through his wife to check with her husband to see if there wasn't something he could do. It was left that way. My first twenty-four hours were about up!

The next day, just as I was off to buy fresh fruit to take on board, I met four policia federal men who had come to look for me at the yacht club. I got Zeca, who had lived in Hawaii and spoke good English, to interpret for me. The upshot was this: if I were to fly out of the country, get a visa and return, there would be no problem in leaving the boat at the yacht club while I was out of the country. On my return, I could be properly processed in. Thus, my visa problem was overcome. I had planned on flying around Brazil while I was there anyway. So I bought a ticket which took me to Bahia Salvador, and then on to Brasilia where I stayed the night. The next morning I flew to the waterfalls of Iguacu, three waterfalls of splendor in central-western Brazil, then on to Asuncion, Paraguay for my visa. I stayed there a few days.

I enjoyed my brief visit to Paraguay. It was fascinating to discover that nearly every intersection in the city of Asuncion lacks a traffic signal! Talk about taking chances walking across the street! Forget it at peak traffic! Cars roll up to the intersection and just keep taking turns melding into the flow or crossing it. It's truly amazing that I saw no accidents while there. They seemed to get on well.

Returning from Asuncion, I landed in Sao Paulo, and then Rio, then hopped to other stops on my way up the coast back to Natal. When I arrived at Natal, I finished my clearance into Brazil. I went to the policia federal first, then on to the port captain. It was not necessary to go to customs since they were closed due to a strike for more money.

In our conversations at the yacht club before I left for Paraguay, I learned a little about the finances of Brazil. ***Most importantly: you cannot get U.S. money in Brazil!*** That includes travelers checks from American Express. You may only charge your credit card in U.S. dollars and then get paid in cruzieros (Brazilian currency) at the official rate. The official rate is one half the black market rate or parallel rate, as it is called there. Oddly enough, the parallel rate is published in the newspaper daily. Brazil is the only country I have visited where this is done. The problem is two-fold. First, being compelled to take the official rate, the tourist is beat one half by not being able to deal in the parallel rate. Second, at the time I visited, Brazilian currency was devaluing by twenty-five percent per month. You certainly do not want to invest large sums in a rapidly devaluing currency! It becomes worthless in buying power very quickly. Can you believe that it is possible to allow inflation to get so far out of control? Each and every month, Brazilians have to contend with a twenty-five percent increase in the prices of everything they buy!

The situation hadn't changed much when I returned in 1993 except that the parallel rate and the official rate were then the same. In 1995, you could buy U.S. currency travelers checks and inflation had decreased.

Forewarned, I made a point of buying American Express ***U.S. currency*** travelers checks in Paraguay. Before being clued in, I had planned on buying them in Brazil. Had I known that they couldn't issue U.S. currency travelers checks, I would have sailed in with them from offshore. Thankfully, because of my friends at the yacht club and my side trip to Paraguay, I was able to get U.S. money at Asuncion this time and knew what to do on later visits.

Within a few weeks in Natal, and after many interesting conversations with my new friends at the yacht club, we developed into a cruising community with Swiss, French, Italian, English, German, American, and Brazilian yachtsmen. English was the predominant language, but there was enough vocabulary from the other languages to add spice to our conversations. This truly international experience provided this insight: people can get along with other people anywhere in the world!

Little did I know it, but destiny awaited me in Natal. One day, I walked to the supermarket for groceries. The store carried a variety of items, in addition to groceries.

While examining an item, I heard a lovely little voice say, *"Excuse me, do you have the time?"*

I turned around to see a small, absolutely beautiful, young woman standing there. The attraction I felt for her was beyond reason or explanation. As I reached into my back pocket for my Portuguese dictionary, my thought echoing in my head was, *"Yes, indeed! Maybe I do have the time!"*

With some hand-waving communication, because her English and my Portuguese were limited, I managed to invite her to go upstairs and have lunch with me in the cafeteria. I later found out that this was the first time she had been in a restaurant. During our meal, I managed to communicate enough to invite her to the yacht club to see ***Mermaid***. Although she had not heard of the yacht club and had no idea where it was, I managed to persuade her to come. After about fifteen minutes aboard ***Mermaid***, she told me she had to go. It was about 1200 LT. She said it was necessary that she return to work. I told her to come again. I'd help her with her English and she could help me with my Portuguese.

Her name was Marione. She was twenty-four years old and I was forty-five. She lived at home with two brothers and three sisters. She had been at the store on a break from her job when she saw me and asked the time. She told me later that she had been watching me for about twenty minutes before approaching me. I was certainly flattered that she liked this old boy so much!

About a week passed. I figured Marione was not coming to see this gringo again. Then one day, there was a knock on the hull. Marione was coming aboard. She had caught a boat ride from the yacht club out to ***Mermaid***. I made some soup for lunch and we worked on my Portuguese for about twenty minutes. Then she had to return to work. This went on for about a month. I couldn't figure out what was going on! I thought she enjoyed my company, but I couldn't pin her down to go out on a date. Nor would she ever say when she would be coming again.

Finally, after several weeks of Marione popping in for our twenty-minute conversations and immediately having to leave, I said, *"It's time we went out for dinner."*

This was on a Friday afternoon. She told me if she stayed, she could not go home. I let this go in one ear and out the other since I figured everyone can go home. We went to dinner, and sure enough, she did not go home. Instead, she stayed Friday, Saturday, and Sunday. She didn't notify her family either. I became concerned about this. There was no problem with her staying on the ***Mermaid***, but I felt that she must let her parents know that she was all right. So she notified her mother and sisters, letting them know where she was and that she was fine. However, no one dared to tell her dad. He ruled the roost with a tight hand to keep his virgin daughters home under lock. At the time, Marione was twenty-four, and her sisters were twenty-seven, twenty-five, and eighteen. All of them respected their father's wishes. I assumed everything was well at the house and that everyone knew where Marione was.

A few days later, Marione's picture was in the paper and she was listed as missing. I got a friend, who could speak Portuguese, to call her dad to tell him that she was alive and well, and that she was at the yacht club. The next morning, we got word that her dad was here and wanted to see us. I took my little lady ashore. We went over to meet her dad. I apologized for his not knowing where she was. I would never knowingly put anyone through the agony of not knowing where his daughter was! Everybody in the family had known but him. Nobody, and I mean nobody, had dared to tell him. Anyway, Marione and her father had a discussion. He tried everything to get her to come home. But she came back and stood by me, hanging onto me, and said, *"No!"*

So what started out as a dinner date turned into a sailing companion for me aboard the ***Mermaid***. It was an amazing sequence of events, almost impossible for this gringo to understand! I made up my mind that this high-spirited young woman, who had taken such a wild leap of desperation and dreams, would not live to regret it. I would do what I could to make sure her dreams came true, so that she would never suffer the tragedy of a dream's failure or the knocks of life that can follow the innocence of youth.

The first thing to do was to get some clothes. Marione had only the outfit she had been wearing that Friday night when it all started. My clothes were doubling for her, but I'm six feet, two inches tall and weigh one hundred and ninety pounds. Marione is five feet and weighs eighty-eight pounds. Shall we say my clothes were large for her? So, off to the store we went. The joy I saw in that young woman's eyes when we bought things she had never dreamed possible, was a warmth in itself. Everything was a first for Marione: her first ride in an elevator, her first long bus ride, her first airplane ride, her first boat ride. I was so used to these things that I didn't think about them. Seeing them through her eyes, they were new again. Sharing her excitement made it exciting for me. Putting Marione aboard the ***Mermaid*** put a whole new dimension into my world trip. It brought this single-hander's heart back to life!

It was getting close to time to sail north. We got a Brazilian passport for Marione. It was important to us that we leave Brazil with good feelings between Marione and her father. The rest of the family was thrilled at the prospects of the adventures ahead for Marione. It wasn't long before her dad gave his blessings, too.

Just before leaving Brazil, Marione and I had dinner with a cruising family. Henry, with his wife and daughter, were working their way around the world. At various ports, they'd work to build up a cruising kitty (saving money). With that in hand, they would head for the next port. While aboard Henry's yacht, we had a lesson in the real basics of insurance. There was a bag hanging in the rigging.

When asked what it was, Henry replied, *"That's our insurance. As long as that bag of dried fish hangs in the rigging, I am confident that my family won't starve to death."*

SAILING THE GUYANA CURRENT

We departed Natal on February 9, 1989. We set sail with the wind east southeast at eight knots. My new sailing companion had eyes as big as saucers. She was already seasick. I tucked her into her bunk to recover, and then planned our route to Port of Spain, Trinidad.

I was determined to stay well offshore in order to pass the mouth of the Amazon River, at least one hundred miles at sea. I figured that would keep us in the Guyana Current while enabling us to take advantage of the trade wind, and to avoid the floating debris from the river. This proved to be true.

I had flown over the Amazon earlier. It was clear to me that the Amazon is no place to have sailing fun. The size of the river and the volume of water flowing down it, is tremendous. It would be difficult to find much but mangrove swamp to tie off to in a very fast current with everything you can imagine coming down the river-not to mention, no swimming! In my opinion, the best way to see the Amazon is to fly to the upper end and catch a ferry going down river. I have always found a river more pleasant when going with the current. Over the years, I've taken two boats down the Missouri and Mississippi Rivers from Omaha, Nebraska to Morgan City, Louisiana. The Amazon makes both of those rivers look like creeks!

A friend once told me of his trip to the Amazon River. He got as far as Belem and cruised around for a bit. His boat has a ***twin keel,*** allowing it to sit on the bottom, straight up, when the tide is out. With this capability, he never worried about getting caught at low tide with no water under his boat. He anchored off an island in the Amazon toward high tide, not leaving enough water under himself for low-tide conditions. When low tide came, there he was, sitting on the bottom with no water under him. He had no qualms because he'd been in this situation so many times before. But when the flooding tide started to come in at his location, it created such a rapid current, that the sand was eroded out from under the boat on one side. His boat was like a rock in the river with rapids running past. It began listing over to an uncomfortable degree with water washing over the rail. Just before it fell over, the water became deep enough for his draft. The boat righted itself. The crisis was over. The change from the precarious situation with rapids on the boat to a tranquil anchorage took about two seconds.

February 10, 1989: The wind was southeast at ten knots with occasional showers.

February 11: The wind was southeast at eight knots.

February 12: The wind was east southeast at five knots. The waves and ocean swell were both southeast and northeast. Our position was 00 degrees 43 minutes south (equator) and 39 degrees 54 minutes west. We had close to two knots of following current.

February 13: The wind was light east southeast and the barometer was dropping. Rain began in the evening. The wind picked up to fifteen knots from east northeast. A petrel landed aboard and rode with us all night.

February 14: The day was cloudy and the wind was northeast at ten knots.

February 15: The wind was east northeast from light air to strong gusts in rain, but a steady breeze of some kind all day and night. The clouds were a high cirrus overcast with altocumulus and stratus to eight-tenths cover most of the day. Our position was 01 degree 46 minutes north and 43 degrees 54 minutes west.

February 16: The wind was variable, mostly east southeast with rain showers and gusts. These rain showers and gusty conditions came from a stratus cloud which was moving west toward the Amazon. The cloud had a crescent-moon shape parallel to the water, or a half-circle shape enclosing us. Around the equator, these storm showers are cold and quick, but the wind from these storms is unpredictable. Some storm clouds carry a good punch like forty knots, and others blow only twenty knots. A good sailor is always on guard for clouds such as these. You must reduce sail each time one comes up! One never knows just how much wind it has. Because of this, day and night around the equator can become a real drag, playing musical sails, up and down, up and down. To avoid aggravation and enjoy my passage, my policy, when in this variable wind condition, is to set the sails for gusting conditions and motor-sail at a low RPM. This moves ***Mermaid*** through the variable conditions with no strain, no pain, and no aggravation with the lousy sailing conditions. I go to sea for pleasure and make every effort not to exhaust myself too badly.

February 17: The sky was overcast with many rain showers. The wind was gusting to thirty knots with a northeast wind steady at fifteen to twenty knots. Our position was 03 degrees 37 minutes north, 46 degrees 48 minutes west. We started to see more flying fish.

February 18, and 19: The cloud cover was overcast to broken with rain showers. The wind was east northeast at fifteen to twenty knots.

February 20: The day was rainy and overcast, but cleared in the afternoon with steady wind from the east northeast at fifteen to twenty knots. Our position was 07 degrees 42 minutes north and 53 degrees 31 minutes west. The barometer was on the rise. We passed the point where the Guyana Current and the Amazon Basin water merges, making the blue water brown. At 1430 LT, ***Mermaid*** went through turbulent waters caused by a current convergence which made a vertical wave chop of about five to seven feet for around twenty miles. Two petrels slept aboard the previous night.

February 21 and 22: The cumulus clouds of the lovely trade wind conditions returned with the wind east northeast at fifteen to twenty knots. The waves were three to six feet with an eight-foot ocean swell. I made good star shots on both days, using Arcturus, Altair, Antares, Spica, and Vega.

February 23: The wind was steady from the east northeast at fifteen to twenty knots. There was some shower activity. Our position was 10 degrees 39 minutes north and 59 degrees 55 minutes west. We closed Trinidad, passing between Trinidad and Tobago, sailing through waters which appeared to be a nursery for flying fish. As ***Mermaid*** broke water with her bow, thousands of small flying fish scattered across the surface. What a beautiful sight!

Marione had survived her first sailing experience, even though at a point, she had thought she might die from her seasickness. I was pleased, and judged that she would become a very good sailor with time and experience.

TRINIDAD

February 24, 1989: We arrived at Trinidad and sailed down the north shore to the east cut. Then we went south through the channel to Port of Spain to arrive at the customs dock. Port of Spain is a pleasant town. It was a good place to pick up visas for Venezuela and Jamaica. There was a law there, which was a first for me! We were required to obtain permission from customs before purchasing diesel fuel or groceries. They retained a customs official on the dock to observe what was brought to the ship. My impression was that they had all the tourist dollars they wanted, and therefore, wanted to make it as difficult as possible for tourists to purchase anything.

We were anchored off Port of Spain with just one other yacht. One evening, we met the couple from the other yacht and invited them aboard ***Mermaid***. He was American and she was Polish. They had been in Venezuela for a year and had cruised that entire area. They strongly recommended that anytime we ordered anything in a restaurant, that we write the prices down as we ordered. Otherwise, when the bill came, the prices might be changed, or other things not ordered added on. Sometimes, the bill might be added up wrong and always on the higher side.

We also discussed language problems. She observed that, like Marione and I, they could barely talk to each other at first because neither knew the other's language very well. She went on to say that now, after two years, she could speak good English. She commented that their relationship had been ***a whole lot better*** before they could communicate so fluently. I suggested to Marione that there was no reason for us to hurry our communications along. Things were really good at the time. So we decided to let our communications develop naturally and not necessarily with great speed.

March 1, 1989: We departed Trinidad and anchored in a protected cove west of Port of Spain.

March 2: We sailed out of Trinidad waters en route to Juangriego, Isle Margarita, Venezuela. This is a fishing village on the north shore of Isle Margarita with a fair harbor. We intended to take a taxi to the southeast end of Margarita where clearance in procedures are handled.

March 4: On our arrival, as we came ashore, we encountered a fellow yachtsman who was trying to buy diesel fuel. The exchange rate at the time was 38 bolivar to $1.00 U.S. Although the official price of the diesel fuel was 2 bolivar per liter of diesel (or about 20 cents per gallon), the marina refused to sell it for less than $1.40 U.S. per gallon! Since we needed gasoline for our outboard and the marina price was ridiculous, I picked up our jerry can and we began to walk toward the gas station, which was about four miles away. There, we could buy gas for about 20 cents a gallon.

As we walked toward the gas station, a pleasant taxi driver who spoke English stopped near us and asked if we needed a lift. This was at a time when a ride to the other end of the island, about twenty miles away, cost $3.15 U.S. Occasionally, I gamble on a taxi driver by not asking about the fare. ***This is always a mistake!*** This time I didn't worry too much because it was only a six-mile round trip from where we were. So we hopped in. As we rode, we had a wonderful conversation with the cabby.

When we arrived back at the marina, I asked, *"How much?"*

He looked me straight in the eye and answered, *"$10.00 U.S.!"*

So within two hours of our arrival, we had observed a fellow yachtsman out of diesel fuel being robbed by a marina fuel dock, and we were robbed ourselves by a taxi driver. That cabby exceeded all my expectations of greed! His greed reinforced my opinion that many cabbies, the world over, are not blessed with integrity, even with a meter. After all, they're the ones who put the numbers in.

We had heard how great it is for tourists in Venezuela. We may have stopped in the wrong place in that country. I'm more inclined to believe we came about three years too late. As a gringo, I expect to pay somewhat more than the locals. That's inevitable. However, due to my foolishness in not establishing a price for the cab fare, and the fact that the cabby took that opportunity to overcharge me, I was furious with myself and Juangriego, Isle Margarita, Venezuela. With this unpleasant experience onshore, we quickly decided that we had had enough of Venezuela. So instead of spending any more time onshore, we rested aboard ***Mermaid*** in the good anchorage for a couple days and then sailed on. Many of our sailing friends have had good experiences in Venezuela.

ACROSS THE CARIBBEAN

March 7, 1989: We departed Venezuela en route to Port Royal, Jamaica. It was a pleasure to be back in the lovely Caribbean. Usually, there is a good east wind, sometimes varying to the northeast or southeast with speeds from twenty to thirty knots in the winter and ten to twenty knots during the rest of the year. It's fantastic sailing! In conditions like these, I make it a general rule never to beat to windward. I may take a long close reach to a landfall. However, if substantial tacking is required, I change destinations. Even having clearance papers showing a different destination from where I arrive doesn't usually prove to be a problem. The papers show where I came from.

I've also found that with a U.S.registered ship, nobody cares much whether the renewal sticker on your documentation is current except the U.S. Coast Guard. An ocean sailing cruiser is truly inconvenienced by the requirement to renew that sticker yearly. Many times the mail is delayed in coming. It really can be a nuisance to have to do this yearly mail exchange with the coast guard. One would think that they could issue permanent documents and save themselves money on the cost of issuing and mailing stickers. With permanent documentation, the boat owner would not have to live under the cloud of threat for not having a current sticker.

It's a very good idea, when offshore, to persuade a friend living in the United States to act as intermediary. He can send the renewal card in at the appropriate time, receive the sticker, and mail it to you at a more convenient time. That way a sailor can sail with the old sticker until a time and place to get the new sticker can be worked out. I'm always reluctant to have the sticker sent to me overseas. The mail service in many countries is not always reliable.

March 13, 1989: It was a beautiful night. We were one hundred fifty miles from Jamaica. After sunset, we saw the

Florida
Ft. Myers Beach
U.S. Coast Guard
Boardings (1989)
During one passage
③
②
①
Gulf
of
Mexico
Straits of
Florida
Key \
Isla Mujeres
82° W
Cozumel
20° N
Mexico
Mexico Navy
Boarding (1989)
Grand Cayman
Chincherro
Bank
Neg
Belize
Roatan
Serranilla
Bank
Rio Dulce
Guatemala
Serrana Bank
Honduras
Roncador Bank
Nicaragua
82° W
Panama
Canal
Costa
Rica
Panama
P

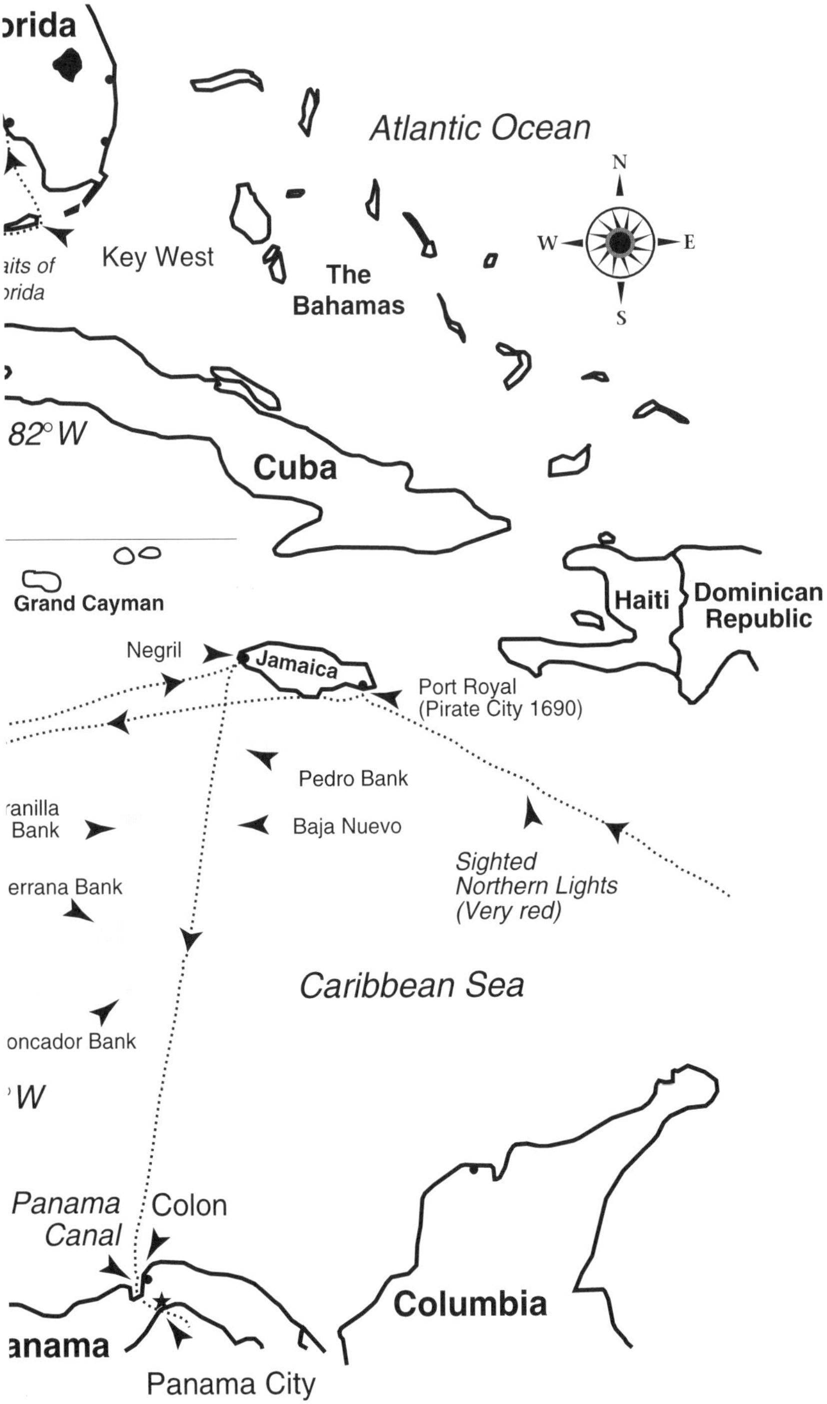

rida
Atlantic Ocean
N
W
E
S
aits of
rida
Key West
The
Bahamas
82° W
Cuba
Grand Cayman
Haiti
Dominican
Republic
Negril
Jamaica
Port Royal
(Pirate City 1690)
Pedro Bank
ranilla
Bank
Baja Nuevo
errana Bank
Sighted
Northern Lights
(Very red)
Caribbean Sea
oncador Bank
W
Panama
Canal
Colon
Columbia
anama
Panama City

brightest, red, northern lights I had ever seen in this area. I had not been aware that they could be seen so far south, but there they were! It is a rare experience to see northern lights in the Caribbean, especially with that intensity.

March 14: *Mermaid* arrived at Port Royal, Jamaica and was boarded by customs. Immigration is at the airport, which is several miles away. So we cleared in there the next morning.

Dropping anchor at Port Royal brought to mind a ***National Geographic*** article I once read concerning the sunken city of Port Royal, which was lost after a devastating earthquake in the 1690's. Our anchor was lying directly over the ruins. The sunken Port Royal was the *"sin city"* of the Caribbean, inhabited by ruthless and homeless pirates. It is not difficult to see why they had picked this location. It is a harbor with two separate channels for sailing in or out. As a rule, the winds favor one channel or the other. In a real emergency, they could have towed a boat to Kingston harbor, which is further up the bay and around a bend, which would have provided even more protection. The old fortifications that guard the bay are still standing.

Port Royal is a convenient, reasonably safe place to anchor a boat. We took the ferry to Kingston for $1.00 Jamaican to go shopping. The exchange was $5.31 Jamaican to $1.00 U.S.

Kingston is an interesting town. Unfortunately, like all big cities, it has its share of thieves. They seem to congregate around the fruit and vegetable markets and the bus stations. They are also found in the crowded streets near the waterfront in the poorer and older sections of town.

On our first trip to Kingston, we were walking toward the market when a fifteen-year-old boy ran up behind us and tried to grab Marione's necklace. She sensed his presence and ducked forward. I saw what was happening and turned toward him. He had a jackknife that he showed me. He flipped it open and shut a couple of times as a warning not to mess with him. Since he was unsuccessful at his thievery, we were happy to let him leave.

A concerned citizen jumped out of his car to assist us, but it was all over before he got there.

A good rule while traveling is not to wear any jewelry. ***Even cheap jewelry*** looks real and ***attracts thieves.***

We continued our shopping. While we were in an arts and crafts market, a fellow approached us to sell us a gold necklace, which was obviously stolen. He may have even stolen it himself. Anyway, we struck up the following conversation with him.

"Why would we want to buy or wear jewelry here when so many people try to steal it when we wear it?" we asked.

"Well, you can buy this jewelry here, and then wear it after you leave Kingston," he replied.

Returning to the ferry, we sat down for the ride back to Port Royal. The seats on the ferry face each other. Thus, you can observe the people sitting opposite you, and they can see you. We were a bit early. The ferry was only half full. The seat next to me was empty, as were many other seats. Not five minutes had passed when a man sat down in the empty seat beside me. In the course of the next ten minutes, he attempted to pick my pocket. A dollar was partially out of my pocket and he saw this. He was gently trying to pull it out of my pocket while I read the paper. Curiously, many of the people sitting opposite us were watching him do this. Not one person said a word! I patiently waited as this went on. Finally, the bill popped out and landed in his lap.

My hand was on the money immediately as I said, *"What are you doing, mon?"*

He jumped up and flashed his jackknife just as the other thief had. When it became apparent that I was not going to threaten him, he left. Not a soul who was watching said anything at all. Later, as he passed through the ferry, he winked at me. I winked back. It was as if he was saying that he was just doing a day's work. No hard feelings!

From that day on, when we went to Kingston, we carried our vegetable bag. Sticking out of it was a three-foot, anchor windlass bar. Many eyes saw the bar. Thieves understood what it was immediately. That seems to be universal anywhere in the world. A potential weapon stops the independent thief. A gang is a different story. Even so, if the gang is small, an open sign of potential resistance encourages them to look elsewhere. We had no more trouble.

I've always liked Jamaica. It can be a really fine, cultural experience. Unfortunately, as with many other places, we have to remember that times can be difficult in a country. When that happens on a large scale, a certain element turns to thievery.

WEST CARIBBEAN

March 29, 1989: We departed Port Royal and headed for Livingston, Guatemala, in order to cruise up the Rio Dulce River. We had a gentle sail with pleasant conditions. We arrived at Livingston on April 5. We had picked up visas in Kingston. That made the paperwork smooth and easy. We had ninety days from immigration, ninety days from customs for the ***Mermaid***, and a ninety-day cruising permit from the port captain.

The Rio Dulce is truly one of the most beautiful places in the world for a cruise! We wound our way up a gentle river between high cliffs and mountains covered with rain forests. Vines overhang the cliffs. There are cormorants, white heron, egrets, and pelicans by the hundreds. The Mayan culture jumped out at us as the dugout canoes went by and as we passed the thatched-roof houses along the shore.

Several miles upstream, the river widens into a lake for about ten miles, and then narrows again into a river. Then it broadens once more into a thirty-mile lake called Izabal. ***It's all fresh water!*** That makes it a good place to wash clothes, and to eradicate the barnacles on the bottom of the boat. In the villages, there is a good selection of fruits and vegetables at reasonable prices. There is also access to many Mayan ruins and to the interior of Guatemala.

While anchored in a lagoon off the river, we had a bit of excitement one night. Marione went topside to look at the moon. As she was looking, she noticed what she thought was one of her ribbons lying on the cabin trunk between the cabin and cockpit. As she reached down to pick it up, it coiled to strike! In about one second, she shouted, ***"Snake!"*** I was topside immediately! The snake moved into the cockpit and coiled around the helm chair pedestal. We later found out that our snake was a small, deadly poisonous fer-de-lance. I ran to get the machete and the flashlight. Marione watched the snake so that we knew where it was. The flashlight didn't work! That delayed me a bit. Finally, I located my twelve-volt light and got it hooked up.

I took it topside and killed the snake with the machete to the great relief of both of us!

The next morning, while discussing our experience with some yachtsmen who live on the Rio Dulce, we learned that there seems to be more snakes washed into this particular bay more often than in any other bay. One yachtsman told us about the time when he had watched a snake come up the bobstay, and go on up the forestay to the top of the mast where it stayed to sun itself. Later, it came back down the forestay and bobstay into the water.

From April 6 until late October, we cruised back and forth between Rio Dulce and neighboring Belize. As an American, I didn't need a visa for Belize, but Marione, as a Brazilian citizen, did. Fortunately, her visa was issued on the spot without a fuss.

The water near Belize is another of my favorite cruising grounds. There are one hundred twenty miles of barrier reef. This makes for many protected anchorages where the gunkholing (that is, short sails between anchorages) and swimming are great!

The combination of Belize and its reefs, Guatemala and its rain forests with freshwater rivers and lakes, and the bay islands of Honduras, together, with the close proximity of the three to each other, makes this area a great cruising ground. It's easy to leave your boat to travel inland to the Mayan ruins or to observe the cultures of the many different tribes that make up the Mayan Indian population. The members of each tribe or clan wear a distinctive design on their homemade clothes, unique to that tribe or clan. It's also easy to clear from one country to another when it becomes necessary to move your boat before import duties are required to be paid. The distances between the various locations are short, an advantage for those into gunkholing rather than long-haul sailing.

While we were in Belize, ***Mermaid*** developed engine trouble. It seemed a good idea to rebuild her engine. I had a parts and maintenance manual. There was also a Perkins distributor in Belize City. It occurred to me that it would be to my advantage to understand my engine one hundred percent, hands-on. Once that engine was rebuilt, you can believe that I did!

Marione and I tore the engine completely down to the block. This made it easy to carry it to a machine shop in order to have new sleeves pressed and bored. All the pieces were in boxes on the cabin sole in front of the engine room, including the crankshaft, the camshaft, and the timing gears. When the new sleeves had been inserted, bored true, and honed to size, we put the engine block aboard and sailed to a nice anchorage ten miles south of Belize City where we proceeded to put the engine with its new parts back together again.

Rebuilding the engine taught me a few lessons. One became very obvious as I worked on the engine. ***A few*** diesel mechanics who charge $40.00 per hour at the marinas simply do not have any in-depth knowledge of engines. The very last time I had hired anyone to work on my engine was in Fort Myers Beach, Florida. I had come into port and anchored under the bridge, and then had brought a mechanic out because the engine would not start. He spent ***six hours*** trying to get that motor started! His procedure in testing an engine was to change the fuel filters, go through the fittings to make sure they were tight, and then attempt to bleed the lines of air. That gentleman had problems with this, so he went ashore and brought a suction pump to pull the fuel through. Still having problems, he decided that the problem must be in the fuel injection pump. He had me towed into the marina. There, I was informed that there would be no dockage charge as long as they were working on my engine. I left the boat there for a week while they had the fuel injection pump rebuilt. It was finally decided that that had been the problem all along. So, the bill for finding out that the fuel injection pump did not work, and to repair it came to $850.00!

While rebuilding my engine, it became clear to me that all the mechanic had had to do when he came aboard was to establish if there was fuel to the fuel injection pump by opening the bleeder on the injection pump, and turning the starter, or using the manual pump. If there is no fuel there, the problem is somewhere before the injection pump. It might be the filters, the fuel pump, or broken or clogged fuel lines. If there is fuel to the injcction pump, the next step is to check and see if there are air bubbles coming out of the bleeder on the injection pump in the fuel. With no bubbles, there are no air leaks in the incoming side of the injection pump. Then the problem has to be in the injection pump, in the injectors (atomisers), or possibly air leaking in the fuel lines on the injector side of the pump.

A good mechanic would then loosen (crack) the injector lines at the injector and turn the engine. With fuel there and no bubbles, the pump and lines are good and the problem is most probably dirty injectors. If there is no fuel after a ***minute*** of cranking, the injection pump is the problem.The worst scenario, if the injectors are good, is that there is no compression. Don't give up hope yet! You can still check to make sure that the air intake is not plugged (look there first) and adjust the valves.

A good mechanic would have taken about a half hour to diagnose the problem with my engine. Removing and installing the pump should have taken about two hours with an additional half hour for travel time. The total bill should have been about $270.00, including $120.00 for the three hours labor and $150.00 for rebuilding the pump, much less than the $850.00 I was charged!

Since rebuilding my engine and learning these lessons, I've never had another mechanic work on any of my engines, including the generator and the dinghy outboard motor. Instead, I buy a parts manual and a maintenance manual for every piece of equipment I buy and do any repairs myself. With the knowledge gained from rebuilding my engine off Belize and doing subsequent repairs, I've become a fair novice mechanic. That gives an extra dimension of freedom in my cruising life. Self-sufficiency is the key to economical cruising. There's a lot of time to learn to be self-sufficient while cruising because the one thing you have when cruising is freedom of time.

MEXICO

We were ready to head for Mexico and the United States. Belize City is a good place to pick up visas for both countries. Our Mexican visas came through very quickly. However, getting a ***U.S. Visa*** for Marione proved to be both an enlightening and exasperating experience. Our attempt to get Marione's visa shed light on why I had been given such a hassle in Brazil. *"Do unto others as they do unto you!"* is apparently the world-wide philosophy concerning visas. Marione and I were not yet legally married at that time. Even though she had $2000.00 in U.S. travelers checks, she was told she had to get her visa in Brazil! I had never experienced such a problem. I had always found that any consulate of any country anywhere in the world should be able to issue a visa for that country. This was the only exception I've ever found.

The problem seems to be that so many Brazilians and Belizeans come into the United States and then simply don't leave. Because of this, U.S. Immigration has clamped down. Even my assurances of support as a U.S. citizen and my offer to take responsibility to insure that she would be out of the country in the allotted time made no difference. Finally, the consulate stamped her passport with a visa for a crewman. I presumed that in doing this, Marione was attached to the boat! To this day, I do not understand why she was not given a normal tourist visa. Immigration in the U.S. is not required to honor the visa and can turn anyone out in forty-eight hours.

Later when we reached Key West, Florida, the visa turned out to be of no value. It was for a hired crewman. By U.S. law, a ***U.S. ship*** can hire only ***U.S. citizens***. Fortunately, an intelligent immigration officer in Key West saw our situation and gave Marione thirty days in the country rather than the normal forty-eight hours. We are forever grateful to him! Not performing as a computer chip, he restored my faith in ***common sense*** and the bureaucrat in the ***U.S.A.***

October 27, 1989: ***Mermaid departed Belize,*** running the coast northward with a mostly east northeast wind. This proved to be a good route once we picked up the Gulf Stream, just as we approached the south end of the Chincharro Bank. We had a beat and then a close reach sailing condition, but were helped greatly by the current. Just north of the Chincharro bank, we were boarded and searched for drugs by the Mexican Navy. They came up to our boat, stopped by us, and had us drop our sails. Apparently, they had not learned that a ***sail increases stability***. As our boat rolled for lack of the stabilizing influence of a sail, they drew nearer in a whale boat with a sailor holding an old tire for a fender, which was supposed to absorb the shock of the boats if they bumped together. However, the tire filled with water and became so heavy that the sailor could not lift it. Consequently, the boats banged against each other. As the boats banged together, one of the two officials managed to step aboard and perform the search. ***"Courtesy begets courtesy!"*** is the rule in such situations. Displaying anger over your boat being smacked by theirs, or over their walking around your nice deck with their hard-soled shoes only creates more problems for ***you!*** Be cool! Smile and assist! They'll be off your boat that much faster!

Continuing north, we passed between the island of Cozumel and the coast of Mexico. As we did, I was reminded of the first time I was afflicted with ***"Montezuma's Revenge,"*** coincidentally in Cozumel. At one time the island was notorious for that problem. Learning from that experience, I now make sure that my first aid kit carries an antibiotic called ***Bactrim***. One tablet has always taken care of the problem for me. When traveling inland, I carry it in my toothbrush kit.

Once we had passed Cozumel, the Gulf Stream really moved us along. We closed to Isla Mujeres, a lovely little island with crystal clear water. Clearance was very easy. All the offices are within a half mile of each other along the water front. We stayed here a short time. Isla Mujeres is a very small island with a couple of roads. The proximity of Isla Mujeres to Cancun has brought a spillover from that resort to this once sleepy, little, fishing village. There are now two big ferries carrying cars to and from this island and Cancun.

THE FURY OF LAND

I returned from the sea
The freedom of the sea
Deep in the Caribbean
I found I wasn't free.

The long arm of Uncle Sam
In a gray ship came to be
They brought their guns
And easily boarded me
I wasn't free.

I had done nothing
Yet I was treated as if I had done something
I was inspected
And I hoped I wouldn't be infected
By this intrusion on the sea.

The gray ship sailed and I wailed
The land of the free how can that be
When you can just come in my home
And roam without cause from me.

COAST GUARD BOARDINGS

November 6, 1989: We plotted a course to Key West, Florida. The next day, we were boarded by the U.S. Coast Guard. We were beating to windward quite briskly in a twenty to twenty-five knot wind when they came over the horizon. They approached and informed us that they were boarding. They understood that leaving the sails up gives a sailboat better stability. As we continued sailing, they ran their twin outboard motorboat with its hard hull and big rubber flotation collar around the top, alongside us, and matched our speed. They laid the flotation collar against our hull, then stepped aboard wearing proper deck shoes. The first few moments of contact are tense for them since they do not know what situation they are getting into. The prudent sailor eases into the confrontation and has everybody aboard topside. Once they are aboard and the tension eases, the search and inspection begins.

When boarded, a sailor must be mindful that the long arm of Uncle Sam and his thumb have reached him. He must not let that free spirit that he has on the high seas interfere with his judgment. As a yachtsman, an American citizen, and a tax payer, I find it definitely infuriating and humiliating for someone to come into my home with no search warrant and treat me like a suspect when I've done nothing to deserve it. But this is the way it is. Remind yourself that these coast guard fellows are pretty nice guys, who are only doing a job that was imposed on them. So, release the tension and assist them in any way that you can. Things will run calmly and smoothly.

I've been boarded many times over the years by the U.S. Coast Guard and have never had damage to the boat or problems with the boarding parties. This time the boarding party made the quickest search I ever had by a team of coast guardsmen. The boat was beating with G-force, and moving so rapidly that if a person wasn't used to it, it could make him seasick really fast, as the boys learned below deck. The officer in charge, while writing up his report in the helm chair topside, excused himself while he vomited over the side. They were so anxious to get off that they jumped together into the bow of their boat. This lowered the boat so far that they took a wave that soaked them all. I suspect that, on that day, they learned just who the ***true sailors*** of the world are!

November 9: We were passing south of the Dry Tortugas Islands, Florida when we were boarded once more by the U.S. Coast Guard. When I showed them the form given to me by the boarding party the day before ***on the same passage,*** they told me it didn't matter. They would perform a search, too. They also said that coast guard boats are not in contact with each other concerning which boats had been searched. That gave me cause to wonder!

The next day we arrived at Key West. We went to the designated marina for customs in order to use the customs phone to call them for clearance. It wasn't working. So I called them on the local pay phone. Once cleared, we took an overnight sail to Fort Myers Beach, Florida, arriving around 0600 LT. We had not even gotten the anchor dug in, as yet another coast guard boarding team was aboard. I showed them the two boarding slips I had. They said they wanted to search anyway. So in our passage from Belize to Fort Myers Beach, we were boarded once by the Mexican Navy and three times by the U.S. Coast Guard. Drug enforcement is necessary, but ***three coast guard boardings in one passage?*** When does it become an infringement of rights for a U.S. citizen?

Just before leaving Belize, while we were anchored in Placencia, we encountered a fisherman with a dinghy for sale. He told us he had found it in the mangroves. It was a nine-foot sailing dinghy with oars and the name, ***Friendly Cove,*** on its stern. I purchased the dinghy from him and left my old dinghy with him. When buying a boat under such circumstances, I always wonder where it really came from. Was it really found in the mangroves or was it found on the stern of, say, ***Friendly***

Cove? Little did I know that I was about to meet the former owner of that dinghy in Fort Myers Beach, Florida.

We had anchored in Fort Myers Beach, Florida and had the dinghy in the water when a boat named ***Friendly Cove*** came in, and also dropped anchor.

I said to Marione, *"Well, I'll be darned!"*

I jumped into our dinghy that still had the name ***Friendly Cove*** on its stern and rowed over to meet the folks.

I introduced myself by saying, *"I believe I have your dinghy!"*

He looked at me and the dinghy and said, *"You do!"*

Over coffee, he told his story. He had been towing his dinghy up the coast of Belize when the trade wind picked up in the afternoon. The dinghy broke loose and was quickly blown into shallow water where he could not retrieve it. Later, in Placencia, he met the fisherman and told him where he had lost the dinghy. Once back in the United States, he filed an insurance claim and was paid for the loss. Just two weeks before I met him and his wife, they had disposed of the original mast, sail, centerboard, and rudder. It reminded me of the saying about being a day late and a penny short.

In my travels, I've met many others who had ***lost their dinghies while towing*** them. It's good practice to put the dinghy aboard in areas with potential choppy conditions and strong wind. Such conditions can prevail almost everywhere.

In December 1989: ***We departed the U.S.*** en route to the Panama Canal. However, with the pending U.S. military action in Panama, we decided to wait and see how that played out before attempting to sail to and through the Panama Canal. So we returned to Belize and Guatemala, and then went on to the island of Roatan, north of Honduras, to enjoy the warm weather.

THE PANAMA CANAL

May 22, 1990: We departed French Harbor, Isla Roatan, Honduras, and beat to windward. When the wind shifted more southeast, we had a close reach to Negril, Jamaica. We had planned a stopover in Negril, but were told that we must go to Montego Bay to clear in. This was a change from previous trips when I'd been permitted to clear out of Negril, as well as into Savannah La Mar on the south coast. The police allowed us to anchor overnight without clearing in. We sailed for Panama on the morning of May 29.

The route to Panama from Negril is fairly direct. There is usually a favoring wind from fifteen to twenty-five knots from the east with a five- to ten-foot wave and an ocean swell to fifteen feet. That makes for great sailing! It is imperative to take a great deal of care to miss the reefs which cover a good part of the Caribbean to the west as a person heads for Panama.

We sailed across the Pedro Shoal, south of Jamaica, with its notorious Banners Reef and very clear waters. We continued on along the east side of the Serranilla Bank, and then between the reef of Bajo Nuevo and Alice Shoal. We stayed as far as possible to the east in order to avoid all the reefs to the west. In addition, I did not want to have to beat back to the east to get to the canal. It was a good sail. Not cutting the reefs too close is always a good idea.

I once knew a fellow with a Valiant 40 sailboat. He came out of Panama, plotting a course through the reefs off Nicaragua. Using his ***satellite navigation*** (Sat Nav), his accuracy proved to be better than the charts. He charted a course to pass a particular reef about three miles to the east. He then set his autopilot to work during the night. The Sat Nav reading that was plotted had him clearing the reef. He woke with his boat pitching sideways in a breaker. Jumping up, he used the engine to reverse course, turning with full power. He bounced three times before he got back into deep water, thus saving his boat.

He immediately plotted his position. It showed he was still clearing the reef. He learned from the experience that a reef may not be precisely where the chart says it is. Now, when navigating with a GPS accuracy, it's really essential to allow for possible inaccuracy in the charted location of a reef, unless the reef's position has been updated on a chart with the ***global positioning system*** (GPS). I always plot a five-mile margin of safety or more when passing reefs and I never close a reef unless it is daylight.

June 4, 1990: ***We closed the Panama Canal Channel*** at 0230 LT. We anchored in a small boat anchorage called the flats off the canal, not far from the yacht club. That very same morning, two friends we had met in Natal, Eric and Rosilyn, arrived aboard ***Wiggy***. We hadn't seen or heard from them in the year and a half since we had left Natal. We enjoyed a wonderful reunion.

Anchoring in the flats on the Cristobal or Caribbean side was a pleasant experience. The water depth of forty feet was a bit deep compared to what we were used to. It's important to become familiar with deep anchorages when going into the Pacific Ocean. The Panama Canal proved a good place to start. Most incoming yachts anchor briefly in the small boat flats to get information. Then they race to the yacht club, in order to secure their boats by Med-mooring (tying stern to the dock, with an anchor forward), and plug into the electric. In addition, most boats are in a hurry to get measured and to transit the canal. They race toward overcruised areas rather than cruising Panama, which still has virgin cruising grounds.

We never had a thief come aboard in the flats. We felt perfectly comfortable in leaving ***Mermaid*** to go ashore. The flats are a mile from the Cristobal Yacht Club. We found the club to be very convenient with a reasonably priced restaurant and hot showers.

The canal organization is a model of efficiency on a scale that boggles the mind. A pilot has an eleven-year apprentice ship to reach the stage where he can handle the largest ships. All pilots must have a second mate's license before they are considered for hire. A top pilot can earn $70,000 a year.

About forty ships a day pass through the canal from all parts of the world and under all flags. One day, a nuclear sub came through, towed by a U.S. Navy tug. I presumed that it was being taken to be repaired or mothballed. The diving planes of the sub were submerged, and consequently, not visible. When a canal tug came to assist the seagoing tug towing the sub, it hit one of the diving planes, which made a hole in its hull below the waterline.

On another day, two World War II vintage liberty ships were being towed through on their way to a scrapping yard. They still had their haze-gray, navy paint. The turret guns were still topside that protected them in the convoy days of World War II. We saw many Panamax class container ships, which are specifically built for passage through the canal. These ships are more than eight hundred feet long and about one hundred feet wide, but draw only thirty-two feet to allow for passage during the dry season when canal depths may be low.

We arrived not long after the U.S. military action in Panama. There were a number of good stories about it going around. The Cristobal Yacht Club is about a mile from the police and customs buildings. During the action, the yachtsmen at the club had a front row view, as five helicopters grouped and flew single file at tree top level over the yacht club, firing rockets and shells into the police barracks. The empty cartridges were falling on the yacht club. The club received only one hit, which may have been from ground fire.

Everyone we talked to in the canal zone had been happy to see the Americans come in! The situation before this action was taken, was truly terrifying to both Americans and Panamanians. There was not one person we talked to in Panama who wasn't relieved that the U.S. had removed Noriega and his Panama Guard from power.

Colon, a city that adjoins the canal zone on the Caribbean side, ***has a bad reputation for thievery,*** which, as we found, is deserved! When one newly-arrived yachtsman walked downtown one afternoon, three fellows walked up to him with knives, demanding his money. We were aware of the problem and exercised caution when we went into Colon. We avoided the big market and also the park area between two streets leading to the market. In other areas of the downtown district, we would cross the street occasionally to check to see if anyone was following us. We never walked under building overhangs with post supports. These offer dark places with little visibility for the police or other pedestrians to observe what might be going on. Many times, we walked along the side of a busy road between the parked cars and the traffic.

While we were in Panama, a step-up campaign to stop the thieves in Colon was underway. When Noriega was in office, his boys had turned a blind eye to the thieves harassing tourists, even thinking it was funny! That gave the thieves the run of the city. Now, with the move to clean up the crime, there seems to be more honest police officers than there were under Noriega. In time, this should help attract tourists to Colon. There is a big duty-free area set up in Colon, which they want to promote.

Our ventures into Colon were mainly to purchase fruit, vegetables, bread, and other supermarket provisions. We also went to the bus station to catch a bus to Panama City, an hour and a half away. The cost was $1.75 in U.S. currency, which Panama also uses as its currency although it is called balboas here. This fare is about the same as taxi fare to Panama City from Balboa on the Pacific side of the country. The ride across the country from either side is pleasant. Panama is a beautiful country. I found most of the people there to be helpful and friendly.

One day, when we were coming out of the bus station in Colon, heading for the yacht club, a fellow around forty years of age approached us. He asked me if I would like a case of pepsi, which was left over from the vandalism that took place during the invasion, for two dollars. I enjoy watching people's reactions, including those of con men.

So I said, *"How nice of you to do me such a favor by selling me your pepsi for two dollars."* I reached into my pocket, took out $4.00, and gave it to him, saying, *"Bring me two cases at the yacht club."*

His smile was huge. He had made his con for the day. He started moving forward, telling me he would hurry and bring the cases to the yacht club quickly. I remember watching that poor, skinny, undernourished thief wearing his heavy, old, army boots running off so happily. I presume that he had worked for Noriega before his demise, perhaps in the Panama Guard. There are not many in Panama now who will hire anyone who worked for Noriega's Panama Guard.

In order to get from one ocean to another, the Panama Canal is probably the best deal in the world! The cost of taking ***Mermaid*** through was under $100 dollars U.S. When you arrive and clear into the country, you also arrange to have your boat measured for the transit, in order to assess the cost. Once this has been done, you need only schedule the transit.

Going through the canal is usually a two-day trip with an overnight stop at Lake Gatun. When scheduling permits, it can be done in just one day. Whether that is permitted depends entirely on the official schedule and the speed of your boat. It is not the usual way to transit a yacht. There are days designated for yachts to go through the canal. Sometimes you raft through the locks, three yachts wide. The canal authorities put an advisor aboard each boat, an apprentice training to be a pilot.

Each yacht is required to have four line-handlers aboard, as well as four, one hundred twenty-foot lines. These lines enable you to center the boat in the lock, with a person on each rope to handle slack as the boat goes up or down in the lock. While we were in Cristobal, we line-handled two boats going through the canal from the Caribbean to the Pacific. Later, when we were in the canal zone at Balboa by Panama City on the Pacific side, we line-handled a boat going to the Caribbean. So, all told, we went through the canal four times.

Line-handlers are very easy to recruit. They can be hired at the yacht club for $40.00 a transit. You can arrange a swap with other yachtsmen, assisting them so that they will assist you. Another option is to call the U.S. military base and offer a soldier a free ride with food and return bus fare. Since our schedule was flexible, I lined up some soldiers who wanted a ride through the canal.

After having a lot of fun in Cristobal, we began the canal transit on August 2, 1990. Our transit was with two other yachts. We rafted in the locks as we lifted to Lake Gatun. We anchored on the lake by ourselves since the other people were in a hurry and had fast boats. The schedule allowed them to make the canal transit in one day.

The next day, we began the drop to come down from the lake to the Pacific Ocean. Rather than center ***Mermaid*** in the lock, we rode the lock side down with fenders and had no problems. Plans must be made around a seventeen-foot tidal change. Oddly enough, while going from the Caribbean in the east to the Pacific in the west, we actually went from northwest to southeast while making the transit. Once out of the last lock, we went under the Pan-American Highway Bridge, and stopped at the Balboa Yacht Club to drop off our line-handlers and pilot.

In Balboa, you can pick up a buoy at the yacht club, continue on to anchor at Taboga Island. Or, as we did, go around the entrance point of the canal towards Panama City. We anchored off the Smithsonian Research Center on the northeast side of the dike that connects with the islands at the canal entrance. This is a favorite anchorage for shrimp boats. There's a small stone and sand beach where a dinghy can be left. We walked down the dike, which has a road on it, and is open to the public. After passing through the toll booth, we caught either a bus or a taxi on our excursions to Panama City.

This was the setting in which I was taken by yet another taxi driver. Throughout my travels I thought I had seen most of the scams. I was seasoned, but this one was new. We flagged a taxi and asked his price to Panama City. He spoke to us in Spanish and Marione and I both understood that the fare was three dollars. When we arrived at Panama City, we handed the taxi driver three dollars. He then said that the fare was six dollars. In the Spanish language, three is *tres* and six is *seis* so they sound very similar. We heard *tres*, but he told us that he had said *seis*. The lesson we learned was to get a written price.

While in Panama, we applied for our cruising permit for Ecuador at their consulate. This takes forty-five to sixty days and cost us two hundred U.S. dollars. The permit would allow us to cruise the mainland and the Galapagos Islands as well, if we desired. However, to cruise the Galapagos Islands, you are still required to have a guide aboard at thirty U.S. dollars a day. It is important to have this cruising permit aboard in Ecuadorian waters. The paperwork is only too often lost between the consulate and, most especially, the port captain's office in the Galapagos Islands. Many cruisers related such experiences, which had caused them annoyance as it held up their cruising plans. While in Panama, we also obtained a visa for Marione to visit French Polynesia.

INTO THE PACIFIC

While waiting for the Ecuadorian permit, we explored the west coast of Panama. To enjoy the Pacific from Panama south to Ecuador or west to Costa Rica, you'd better be a motor-sailor! The ocean is so blue and calm that I couldn't believe it! There is always a swell, but it is not very large. The wind is variable and unsteady. The cruising is fabulous, but don't plan on sailing unless you want to take a lot of time.

We explored the Chiriquie area of Panama to the northwest towards Costa Rica. Here is more virgin cruising country. In this area, we saw many sea snakes coming to the surface. Sea snakes are venomous marine snakes with finlike tails. These particular sea snakes were not large, perhaps two feet in length. They were green with red and yellow spots.

One anchorage that stands out in my memory in this area is Bahia Honda. This is a lovely anchorage with high hills encircling the bay with a waterfall cascading down one hill. There is an island centered in the bay which has a small village on it. While we were anchored off the village, many native children rowed their dugout canoes made from logs out to ***Mermaid*** to trade and to visit. They would bring an egg, a coconut, a banana, or a mango and trade it for a pencil, a piece of paper, or a magazine. It was great fun. By the time we sailed, I am sure we had supplied the local classes in school with paper, pencils, and National Geographic magazines, firing their imaginations to the outside world.

Next, we went to the Las Perlas Islands. These islands are a part of Panama. They are wooded with great rock beaches and, usually, white sand. When that large tide is out, some of the islands have great beachcombing for shells and are great for walking on. The water is clean with good underwater visibility for snorkeling.

Contador is the most northerly of the group. This is where the Shah of Iran took refuge when he was overthrown. His memory is still very fresh with the natives. They told us they had been very frightened while he was on their island. So many people were trying to get at him in order to kill him. Security was in force at all times.

In most anchorages in the islands, there is usually a Pacific swell that rolls a bit. Seldom did we see anyone at all. Yet, the lesson I've learned in sailing is that there are ***always eyes on you*** from the shore. Occasionally, they are thieving eyes. Taking precautions always pays!

A friend once related an experience he had had while he was anchored off a lovely key near the Belize Reef. Because it seemed to be such a remote area, he left his boat open while he took his dinghy to a reef a mile away. Since he could see his boat, he felt comfortable diving there. After a while, he noticed a fishing dory had come in, but did not appear to be close to his boat. It was off to the right a bit, but seemed further away. What he learned was that depth perception is lost with distance, making the dory seem to be further away than it actually was. When he returned to his boat, he found he had been robbed.

Yet another yachting friend recounted how, while at Thursday Island, Australia, he went ashore with his crew, leaving his boat open and unattended. An opportunist happened to go by and stole all the clothes and cameras aboard. One crew member had made the mistake of ***"hiding"*** her passport in her clothes, so it was stolen as well. As people often do, she had put it in a pocket and pushed it to the bottom of the drawer so that no one would find it-or so she thought! The lesson they all learned was that, in the third world, the very clothes we take for granted are top priority for thieves. It would be better to find a different hiding place and to lock your boat!

It would be great to cruise the Las Perlas Islands with people on another boat. You could take turns watching the boats at anchor, giving both the opportunity to really explore these remote islands.

We cruised between the Las Perlas Islands, the island of Taboga-another part of Panama, and the Smithsonian Institute Research Center anchorage. We anchored at Taboga a number of times. The anchorage here was a bit rolly from the ocean swell. This anchorage is used by the tuna fishing boats. A refrigerated ship anchors here until fully loaded with tuna by these boats.

There is a scheduled ferry that runs between Taboga and Panama City. We did not go on it but many cruising boats that do not want to pay buoy fees at the Balboa Yacht Club, or who have not thought of anchoring by the Smithsonian Research facility go to Taboga to anchor. They use the ferry to get to Panama City to clear out of the country of Panama.

We enjoyed hiking at Taboga. We found an old road that we followed along the ridge of a hill that allowed us to reach the top. We had a good view of all the ships in the Balboa flats waiting to transit the canal. We could also see Panama City on the mainland.

THE CRUISING WOMAN

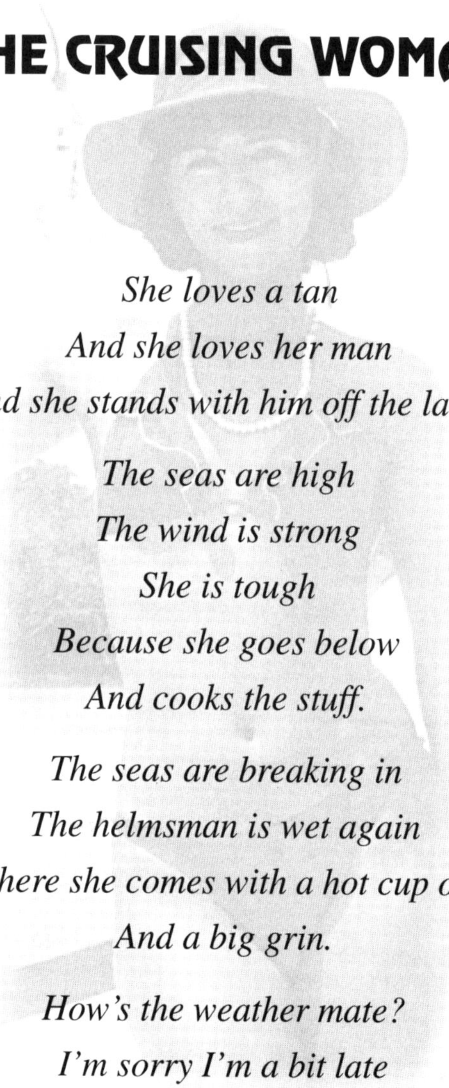

She loves a tan
And she loves her man
And she stands with him off the land.

The seas are high
The wind is strong
She is tough
Because she goes below
And cooks the stuff.

The seas are breaking in
The helmsman is wet again
And here she comes with a hot cup of tea
And a big grin.

How's the weather mate?
I'm sorry I'm a bit late
But the bloody spaghetti
Fell off the plate.

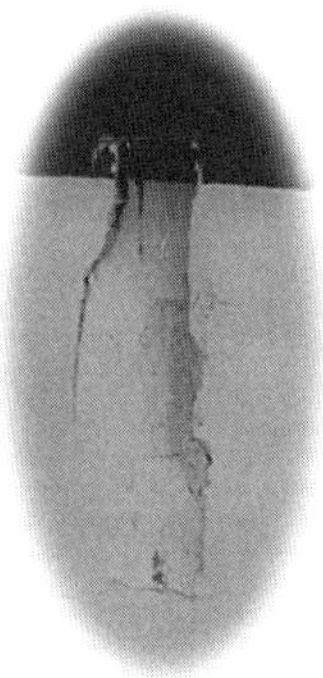

COLLISION

The day was clear, the sun was bright
Everything should have been all right
The old man came from the sea
In his fruit boat of thirty-three
His eyes coated so white
You knew he had spent his life
On the sea so bright.

He headed direct for the dock
And ran through the anchorage without a thought
Slamming into MERMAID'S side
and coming to a halt
Then falling on the deck with a summersault.

The bang like a shot woke me to thought
I looked out the hatch and saw what was his fault
He said he couldn't see and would be back
As I watched the man make fast track
And knew he would never come back.

GOLFITO, COSTA RICA

November 18, 1990: We departed Panama on our way to Golfito, Costa Rica. The wind was from the northeast. There were rain squalls that lasted for six hours. For the balance of the day, the wind was light and we motor-sailed.

November 19: It was a beautiful day! The wind was five knots or less and we motor-sailed.

November 20: There was a five-knot wind and a current on the bow. We motor-sailed.

November 21: We beat to windward in fifteen to twenty knots of wind on a course of 300 degrees true with a preferred course of 310 degrees true.

November 22: We sailed close to the wind all night, then later, we motored on a direct course in a five-knot wind or less.

November 23: The wind was from the west northwest at eight knots. We were sailing close to the wind in a gentle sea with warm, pleasant breezes. We were about ten miles from the Costa Rican border and from our turn north into the Golfo Dulce Bay. A U.S. Navy frigate closed us just as we were enjoying the sunset. They boarded us for a drug search and inspection. Even though it was a naval ship, the boarding party was made up of coast guardsmen who were riding on the naval vessel. To the coast guard, this is known as ***"riding the gray boats."*** While the coast guardsmen were performing their search, the navy contacted them and inquired if they would like them to launch a boat with divers to inspect the bottom of ***Mermaid.*** The coast guardsmen did not feel it was necessary and so declined their offer.

November 24: We motored up the bay to Golfito in calm waters with a light breeze picking up in the afternoon from the northwest. One can depend on showers and possible thunderstorms at Golfito every afternoon. We arrived after the rain at 2100 LT. There was a full moon for assistance in closing the channel which was new to us.

Golfito is on a well-protected lagoon off the Golfo Dulce Bay. Clearance in is easy and efficient. This is a stopping place for many cruisers, a meeting place for old salts and new adventurers. This made a good mix for conversation and sea stories. Nearly everyone from California going to the Caribbean stops here as do those going toward California from the canal.

Here, we met Shane Atkins, the author of ***Super Shrimp.*** He had sailed around the world in a ninteen-foot boat made of three-eighths inch plywood-a real adventure! Dick Munzer, on his ***Marco Polo,*** a three-master he had built and had just finished an eight-year circumnavigation on, was resting there. Dwight Haskins, who had single-handed around the world some years before, had now settled in Golfito. There was another fellow in a twenty-five-foot sloop, who would finish his circumnavigation when he got to Hawaii.

Every morning at twilight, the howling monkeys begin their howling. If you have not heard howling monkeys, you will be impressed! Their noise sounds like ***King Kong*** is about to come out of the jungle. When I actually saw the monkeys, I wondered how all that noise could come out of such little animals!

Theft of dinghy motors, as well as of dinghys, themselves, is a problem in Golfito. One must be very careful. It is one of the few areas I've been where there are so many twenty-five foot runabouts pushed by two- to five-horsepower engines of every make in the world that I could think of. One yachtsman anchored off the town during the day and went ashore, leaving his boat open. When he returned just an hour later, all his camera equipment had been taken. Shane told us he once had had a one-man, rubber dinghy that leaked so badly that every time he went to shore, he had to blow it back up in order to return. One night, even though it was half deflated, someone made off with it.

We anchored off the northwest end of the lagoon, off Tom's place and Dewight's Restaurant. About 1100 LT, while we were below, a twenty-six foot fruit boat ran into us broadside. All of a sudden, ***"Bang!!"*** It sounded like a gun had gone off. I jumped topside to see what had happened. I saw the bow of a boat rammed into the middle of ***Mermaid's*** side. The old man who had been operating the boat, which had just run into us, had been knocked onto the deck. He was getting up while trying to reverse his engine to back off. As he backed off, it became obvious that ***Mermaid*** had a hole in her the shape of his stem timber. It was about a foot long and four inches wide, about four feet above the waterline.

"You put a hole in my boat!" I said to him.

"I can't see!" was his reply.

Looking at him, I had to agree that he couldn't see. He was very old. His eyes were a very milky blue, covered with cataracts. He said he'd be back, but never returned. I didn't pursue him. My friends onshore told me to notify the port captain, who would make him pay for the damage. But how do you get money out of someone who doesn't have any? Had I waited for the money, or to find someone to repair the boat, I'd be waiting for a hundred years! I didn't feel that the potential aggravation would be worth the trouble. As bad luck would have it, he had hit ***Mermaid*** exactly in the middle of the space between two ribs, which is the least-supported part of the hull. I fired up the generator, got out my power saw, drill, planer, belt sander, planking, and fiberglass, and repaired it. I had it sealed before it rained that day.

We saw that fruit boat a couple of other times during our stay. He was well away from us, staying in the channel. Sadly, he never had the courtesy to apologize for ramming ***Mermaid.***

A good place to anchor in Golfito is the Jungle Club, owned and run by Whitey and Barb, on the southwest side of the lagoon. They have a friendly restaurant, which is a meeting place for yachtsmen. They also offer all the services yachtsmen need at a fair price.

It was safe to leave our boat anchored at the Jungle Club. Whitey lined up someone to sleep in the cockpit to keep thieves away at night. This made it possible to leave the boat, and take a bus trip to the capital, San Jose, and to see the countryside along the way.

Costa Rica is a lovely country with its lush, green, mountain slopes. There are many terraced mountainsides with pineapple and coffee plantations. San Jose is an interesting town with a healthy climate. It seemed good to us to be in a drier environment, since Golfito is so humid. While there, I had hopes of getting my sextant mirrors resilvered. The salt air had finally started to break them down. The silvering was all coming off. It was amazing that the mirrors worked at all! I had no luck in the silvering department. So I stopped at a glass dealer who handled regular mirrors. I thought, *"Any mirror is better than no mirror."* I asked if two mirrors could be cut like those I handed him. One was a rectangular mirror, the other, round with one-half clear. He said he could do it.

I asked *"How much?"*

It worked out to $1.00 U.S. I later installed and adjusted them in my sextant and all was well. I navigated around the world with these mirrors, and I am still using them at this writing in 1995.

The exchange rate while we were there was 92 to 103 colons to the U.S. dollar. We had thought supplies in Costa Rica would be less expensive than in the United States, but found that they were comparable. Contrary to the impression of many Americans, that's very good! It takes only a world trip to see how really good our prices are on everything. We even have the nerve to demand service and get it with a smile, something you don't see in much of the world.

In San Jose, sea turtle eggs were being sold in the streets. Considering the scarcity of sea turtles, this seems a shame. But, life is contradictory. Coming through the Grand Caymans in 1993, we passed a facility where they had raised green turtles and loggerhead turtles. They were closing it down in response to international conservation pressure. Because they sold the turtle meat to restaurants, the claim was that they were creating a taste for turtle meat. Therefore, they shouldn't raise them. Believe me! There is already a taste for sea turtle meat all over the world. It's a shame that that facility is shutting down. It was also stocking the sea with more turtles. In my opinion, the only people that dream of saving a species are those with enough money and food to care.

We met a tourist who was about fifty years old, who had been robbed in San Jose. I don't mean to talk so much about thievery. Yet, I feel it is wise to understand the many different approaches to being robbed. It helps a person avoid it while traveling.

As this particular gentleman walked down the sidewalk one day, an attractive woman ran up to him and threw her arms around him with a broad smile. Then, she reached into his pocket as if to flirt with him, while really she was just getting her hands on his money! Next, she pulled her hands out, ran to a waiting car, jumped in, and they drove off. All of this happened very fast. He didn't have time to think and wound up ***$100.00 U.S. short.***

One has to wonder why any tourist carries so much money in one place, or even at all, while walking in town. Why does a yachtsman walk away from his boat or dinghy, leaving it open and unsecured? Is it just wishful thinking that everyone is honest? Or, is it just inexperience with the real world, a world where a five-horsepower dinghy motor can represent a half-years pay for many people? Thinking about this makes one wonder why there isn't more thievery. However, most people are honorable. This makes traveling worthwhile, as you meet them, and see their cultures. Yet there are certainly thieves everywhere that you travel. You must be alert for them.

When we boarded the bus back to Golfito, it had become chilly. The warmth of the lower elevation felt good. It was getting close to the time we had set to sail to Ecuador. Before we left, we wanted to paint the bottom of the ***Mermaid.***

Golfito has a nine-foot tidal change, making it a good place for working on the bottom of a boat. Our only problem was that the shore where we wanted to lay ***Mermaid*** over was covered with small stones, which could gouge her sides. We solved this problem by filling some bags with sand. As ***Mermaid*** laid over that last bit, we shoved the sandbags under the hull. This provided a couple of supports for her to lean against to avoid direct contact with the stony ground.

Careening a boat is a great strategy when working on the bottom. You're working against a side rather than being under the boat and having to reach up. Yet one more reason I love ***Mermaid*** so much is that her long keel is perfect for careening. We soon had the boat painted and were soon ready to move on to the next leg of our journey.

ON TO ECUADOR

January 14, 1991: We departed Costa Rica en route to Salinas, Ecuador. We started out at 1815 LT and beat windward into a south wind shifting to west.

January 15: Our course was 167 degrees true as we sailed in a light wind. Later, the wind picked up to fifteen knots from the southeast, moving to the northeast. The sky was completely overcast and there was heavy rain.

January 16: It was calm with a southwest swell and overcast. At 1700 LT, the wind blew up to fifteen knots from the south with ***Mermaid*** beating to windward. We sighted two blue-footed boobies which are white with black wings, and some brown sea gulls.

January 17: We sailed most of the night with a ten-knot wind from the southwest. The wind shifted from the south to the west during the day. The day started out calm in the morning. Later, the wind built up from the south, then shifted from south to west by evening. Great sailing! Our position was 05 degrees 08 minutes north, 82 degrees 44 minutes west. As we sailed onward, it became clear that we had taken a good route to Ecuador by starting our sea passage from Costa Rica. Had we started directly from Panama, the wind and sea would have been on our bow.

January 18: The southwest ocean swell increased. The wind was light so we motor-sailed.

January 19, 20, and 21: The wind was five knots from the southwest and our course was 195 degrees true. We saw a frigate bird with a white throat and a tropic bird. Our position was 00 degrees 06 minutes south and 80 degrees 42 minutes west.

January 22: We passed Isla de Plata at 1330 LT. Our course was 160 degrees true. The wind was light. We were motor-sailing and sighted our first Ecuadorian fisherman in a single-motor dory, thirty miles offshore.

January 23: We arrived at Salinas in the morning. Clearance was straightforward and quick, since we had the right paperwork in hand. The anchorage at Salinas is open to the north, but gives good protection from the southwest swell. Usually, there is very little wind. Indeed, Ecuadorians use the Pacific as if it were a lake. That's how calm it stays in that region. Once during our stay, we had a north swell for about three days, but with no wind.

To our surprise and delight, the anchorage filled up with old friends, none of whom we expected to see. Among them were Eric and Rosilyn, British, on ***Wiggy,*** whom we had met in Natal, Brazil and had last seen in Panama six months earlier; Henry and Isabelle, French and Swiss, on ***Kim***, last seen two years earlier in Natal, Brazil; Philip and Leonora, Australian and Peruvian, on ***Pompero II,*** last seen in Las Palmas, Canary Islands; and Dave and Elki, British and German, on ***Strawberry Dragon,*** last seen in Panama three months earlier. We enjoyed a regular old home week with plenty of story swapping.

Philip and Leonora told us that ***Pompero II*** would have been well into the Pacific, finishing her eight-year circumnavigation, had she not started taking on water a few days into the Pacific. They returned to Esmereldas, Ecuador to replace some planks. That done, they stopped in Salinas on their way offshore once again.

Dave and Elki related a scary mishap they had had when they almost lost their vessel on the way to Salinas. They had left Panama and were beating to windward, one tack toward shore, then one tack toward the sea. It was a black night and, where they were, the Colombian shoreline was a black shore. Dave took a tack toward shore and sailed on, not realizing how close he was to that black shore, since there was no visual help. He had taken a celestial position, but the currents had apparently given him unexpected set and drift. His ***margin for error*** hadn't been sufficient. They hit a reef off the Colombian coast. Dave dropped the anchor, but ***Strawberry Dragon*** laid over, and was working on the reef with the incoming breakers. The ride in the breakers was extremely rough. It was all they could do to get their dinghy into the water to ride toward shore. Dawn was coming up as they reached the shore. They could see and hear their boat working on the reef. Trying to figure out what to do and not being able to stand hearing their boat scraping on the reef, they walked down the beach and around a point.

About an hour later, they came back around the point to see the boat. It was standing upright in the water! They rushed to their dinghy, which had sustained some damage while getting away from the sailing vessel. They pushed it back through the waves, now breaking on the shore, and rowed back to their boat.

Once aboard, they found that the engine had gotten wet. Dave couldn't get it started immediately. So, they took another anchor out with the dinghy and kedged their boat into deeper water. They were lucky! They had hit the reef at a low flooding tide. The flooding tide and ***the fact that they had dropped an anchor*** saved their vessel.

Now, they had to figure out what to do. The rudder was bent over and the boat could not be steered. A fisherman in a dugout happened to come by. Dave asked if there was any protected place or harbor where they could put their boat. The fisherman replied that there was a river mouth close by where he kept his boat, and a nearby village.

The fisherman left to get help to tow them in. An hour later, thirty motor-powered dugouts appeared. Dave hired two of them to tow them, as he didn't want to pay thirty people for a tow. When the boat was in the river, the village men helped Dave get the rudder off. They built a big fire, then threw the steel rudder on it. They hammered it as straight as they could and put it back on the boat. Dave and Elki stayed in the village a couple of days. They gave the villagers almost all of their clothes and then sailed for Salinas.

Can you imagine how you would feel in a remote area of Columbia with thirty unknown dugouts coming at you? Their experience reaffirms that human nature is basically good. Perhaps mankind does have a chance to survive on this planet in peace one day.

You might also draw the conclusion that it is not good practice to tack toward shore at night! This is especially true when your distance offshore is not great, the shore is dark, and the ocean depths so steep to the shore, you have no help from soundings. Of course, you might just switch the GPS on to determine latitude and longitude. But what if that doesn't work? I know, just turn on the radar! And if...? There is just no limit to the alternatives available to the cruiser who is willing to spend the money to purchase and maintain electronics. For me, there is no greater satisfaction than in sailing around the world with some type of sextant in hand, like James Cook, Joshua Slocum, or any of the other great adventurers of history. Even with our modern tables and sextants, celestial navigation allows you to experience some of the feelings they had to have experienced and puts you closer in touch with the original adventurers.

Ecuador was enjoyable. We were glad that we opted to go directly to the mainland where the cruising isn't spoiled by all the regulations and rackets, as we had heard the Galapagos Islands region was. That kept our perspective fresh in the under-cruised area, where we could sail without annoyance.

In Salinas, the fruits and vegetables are great, plentiful, and reasonable in cost. However, the most outstanding treat was the catch of the sea. At the market, we could select from the fresh daily catch of dorado, cortina, lobster, shrimp, prawns, stone crab, oysters, squid, octopus, tuna, and others that I was not familiar with. In Ecuador, they still fish with the less costly and less efficient methods, leaving some fish for another day. That means that the locals have wonderful fish at very good prices such as one dollar U.S. per kilo (2.2 lbs).

We loaded diesel there for 39 cents a gallon, since they produce oil in Ecuador. The exchange rate was 920 to 1030 sucre to $1.00 U.S.

We took the bus to the city of Guayaquil where the Guayaquil River runs. The famous archaeologist, Thor Heyerdahl, floated his balsa logs down this river en route to Peru to build his raft, ***Kon Tiki.*** He then drifted and sailed with the wind and current to the Marquesas Islands.

We stayed in a lovely hotel for $5.00 U.S. The next day, we flew to Quito aboard a 727. The thirty-minute flight cost us $18.48 U.S. That price had been raised by forty percent just three days previously. Always a day late and a penny short.

Quito is at a nine thousand-foot altitude. The air is a bit thin. We didn't run a lot here. The vegetable and fruit markets are great with produce grown and sold by the Indians. I was so fascinated by the market of plenty that I decided to take a picture of it. As I was getting my camera ready, an old woman threw an ear of corn at me. That reminded me that she and the others thought that being photographed would steal their spirits away, a common belief among the Indians in Central and South America. I simply walked down the street, put a 600mm lens on my camera, and took my pictures from a less obvious spot. This made us both happy. I got my pictures and the Indians didn't know that their pictures had been taken.

Quito is a beautiful city and an interesting experience only a stone's throw from the equator. If you'd like to have your picture taken while standing on the equator, here is a good place to do it. Standing on the ***Mermaid's*** deck was good enough for us.

On our return to Guayaquil, we decided to stock up on canned goods and other provisions for our Pacific passage. Guayaquil is a good place to provision. With our supplies purchased, we had to find a taxi to take us the forty miles back to Salinas. I must say, I wasn't impressed with the condition of the tires on any cab I saw. We finally found one that seemed adequate and so we negotiated the deal. Then, we loaded the car, completey filling it. There was just enough room for the driver and me, with Marione sitting in my lap in the front seat. As we raced down the road in an overloaded car, going sixty miles per hour, I had great misgivings about those bald tires. Now, there are bald tires with black rubber and there are bald tires thread-bare with very little rubber left. This cab had the ***third*** type! I couldn't figure out how a tire that bald could keep air inside it. I suspect there was an inner tube inside that tire that was thread-bare as well.

As we tore down that road, we hit a wet spot. That car took a 360 degree and then a 180 degree loopity-loop before it could be stopped. Amazingly, we were unharmed. There were deep ditches on both sides of that road, and luckily no cars were coming in either direction. A trip into one of those ditches or an oncoming car would have ended or slowed down our trip. Luckily, all was well.

We continued racing down the road. The cabby had, apparently, learned nothing from his near accident. I had to slow him down with the incentive of a couple of extra bucks. We were between towns. I didn't want to end up taking out all the provisions and sitting by the side of the road.

Arriving safely in Salinas after all, we unloaded that cab and settled our bill. As I was picking up groceries and Marione was leaving the cab, the cabby told her that he loved her. She told me what he had said as we hauled our groceries to the dinghy. With a young lady as pretty as Marione, the young bucks swarm as much as flies in an open air meat market.

SAILING WITH EL NINŌ

Eric and Rosilyn were the first to sail. They intended to make a brief stop in the Galapagos Islands, though they had no permit papers. One boat skipper I talked to went without a permit and was allowed a five-day stay. Later, they were to go on to Easter Island and Pitcairn Island. Their travel plans were influenced by all the various writings on the great places.

In planning our itinerary, Marione and I were more strongly influenced by how good the harbor is wherever we were headed. We figured that every place was new to us. There are a lot of nice places. We look for good harbors. We prefer one-time British territories many times. The British left behind them organized governments and viable local economies, and had territories all over the world. A rule of thumb: former British possessions usually have reasonable prices and viable local economies, French possessions are usually very expensive, while former Spanish and Portuguese possessions usually have a low per-capita income and, often, rapid inflation.

If you bring a strong offshore currency, you can live very economically in some former Spanish and Portuguese colonies. These also have fine fruit and vegetable markets, thanks to the local Indian and mulatto population. However, change is in the wind. One has to look harder for an economical country. Some countries we have found and liked are Guatemala, Ecuador, Paraguay, American Samoa, Fiji, Mauritius, South Africa, Brazil, and the United States of America. The United States can provide you with anything that is made anywhere in the world. The prices on material things are as good as anywhere in the world, and usually better than most other places.

March 23, 1991: ***We motored out of Salinas*** in a flat calm (the condition in that area most of the time). We were en route to Hiva Oa, Marquesas Islands. Our general heading was southwest to west southwest and we were motor-sailing with a small southwest swell and a four-knot wind. Our sailing plan was to drop to the southeast trade wind south of 5 degrees south latitude, going however far south we had to go to get to good wind. On that very first day, we sighted three sea turtles and six whales.

March 24: The wind was south at seven knots with seas from the south. We were sailing with main and genoa, and saw many small squid and one sea turtle. There were also many terns, white birds with black stripes on their wings.

March 25: The wind was south to south southeast at ten to twelve knots. I took a good star shot with Canopus, Pollux, and Capella. Our position was 03 degrees 41 minutes south and 84 degrees 13 minutes west. That day we sighted a blue-footed booby, sea gulls, and three Wilson petrels, which are small birds with brown and white markings. With the south southeast twelve-knot wind, the three-foot waves, a west southwest course, and a three-quarter moon with a clear sky, our sailing was as good as it gets!

March 26: The wind was east southeast at five knots and we passed through a very non-rhythm sloppy sea (waves going every direction). Our course was 205 degrees true. We sighted two tropic birds with their orange beaks, white color with black trim and beautiful long tail feathers.

March 27: We had great sailing with the southeast trade wind blowing at twelve to fifteen knots. Our course was 250 degrees true.

March 28: The wind held south southeast at twelve to fifteen knots. Our course was 265 degrees true with a 5 degree east variation correction. We sighted a sea turtle and about fifty dolphins ran with us for a time. Our position was 05 degrees 58 minutes south and 88 degrees 46 minutes east. Toward evening, eight pilot whales, most of them about twelve feet long, came in and ran with us as we sailed. The whales were huffing and puffing to stay alongside. They were very close to the hull, almost rubbing on ***Mermaid's*** bottom at amidships. Those whales, using all that power, made me nervous, since they were so close together on both sides of ***Mermaid*** at the flattest part of her bottom at the beam.

I remembered a magazine article I had read prior to sailing. It told of a sailboat which was sunk by whales some 1,500 miles southwest of Costa Rica. Small whales had come in beside the boat, then bigger whales. Soon, there were more than a hundred running alongside. The sailor heard a bump on the hull, then another, and another. By that time, the boat was taking water and he abandoned ship. He remarked that they were swimming on all sides of his boat, giving him no where to turn.

I wondered just how the whales would react if we simply stopped sailing and ruined their fun. Concerned about the damage they could do to ***Mermaid***, we dropped sails and simply drifted. This got amazing results! The whales apparently didn't know what to make of our stopping. They dropped about a hundred feet behind us and formed into a circle on top of the water. We could imagine their conversation, as they just stopped there. After about five minutes of this, I pulled up the jib and we attempted to sneak off. No way! One of them saw us and came back to play. The others followed his lead and were on their way back as well.

We dropped the sail once more. They returned to their drift position. I started the engine and turned perpendicular to our original course, motoring away. Not long afterward, we could almost sense them reaching a unanimous decision: this is strange behavior! Let's get out of here!

Once we seemed to be safely away from the whales, we pulled the sails back up, shut down the engine, and resumed our original course. We didn't see them again. I think that the whales didn't leave out of fear of the motor, since they left in a leisurely fashion. It just seemed that they decided that this was just too strange. I've had pilot whales run with me over the years many times but never just under the amidships like these.

PHOTO DESCRIPTIONS

1. Bill Spooner and I pouring lead with an eight- and a five-pound ladle. We found out the clamps to hold the mold were not necessary. The lead cooled and contracted so fast there was little pressure on the sides.
2. Drilling and bolting the outside ballast to the eight by twelve-inch Douglas fir keelson. It was bolted on with one inch stainless steel bolts alloy 316.
3. Standing ***Mermaid's*** backbone.
4. Drilling white oak flooring with leader holes to drive five-eighths inch galvanized drift bolts that were 17 inches long.
5. Sawn white oak ribs fastened with seven inch galvanized nails at the rabbit line. Then bolted to the oak flooring with three-eighths inch galvanized carriage bolts.
6. ***Mermaid*** is beginning to grow. Her lofting is in the background.
7. The engine was put in early to gain room in the shop. The shaft hole went through thirty-six inches of Douglas fur.
8. I'm feeling good, "But it's a long road to the end of this project!"
9. Western red cedar strip planking. When the job was completed ***Mermaid*** used 50 pounds of bronze nails vertical, 2800 bronze two and one-half inch wood screws, and 25 gallons of 3M-5200 sealant between rib and plank, and between planks.
10. ***Mermaid's*** hull was covered with three layers of fiberglass cloth with white pigment in the resin on the last two layers.
11. Refining the independent system to raise and lower ***Mermaid's*** mast.

12. Getting ***Mermaid*** ready to truck to the Gulf.
13. ***"Whew!"*** she is finally ready to go to the sea.
14. ***Mermaid*** at sea.
15. Rebuilding the Perkins 4-108 in ***Mermaid's*** engine room.
16. Coast guard boarding in the Yucatan Channel.
17. Marione showing off her red hat.
18. Marione showing off her white hat.
19. Marione, weighing only eighty-eight pounds, makes our nine-foot dinghy look very roomy.
20. Our adviser going through the Panama Canal.
21. This snake boarded us while anchored in the flats at the Panama Canal.
22. The hole left in ***Mermaid*** after being hit at anchor in Golfito, Costa Rica.
23. Careening ***Mermaid*** held up with sand bags on a rocky shore in Golfito.

1

4

2

5

6

3

7

8

9

13

12

10

11

14

17

15

18

16

19

23

21

20

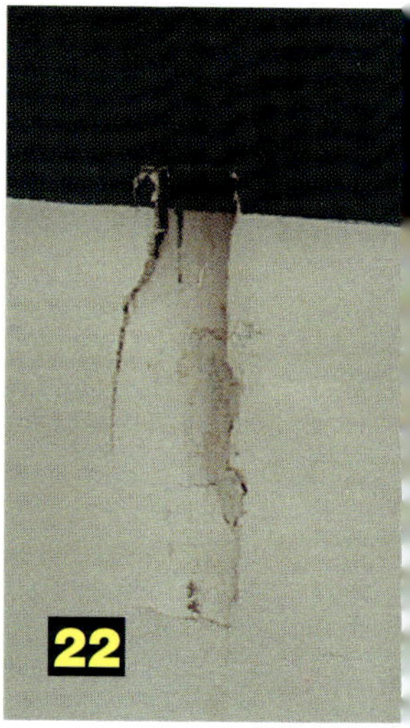
22

24

25

26

27

28

29

35

32

33

PAUL
GAUGUIN
1903
31

30

34

36

40

37

39

38

41

44

46

45

47

43

42

24. Indian fruit market in Quito, Ecuador.
25. Marione washing clothes by hand with a smile.
26. Henry (Swiss), Isabelle (French), and their daughter, Alisia, aboard their yacht, ***Kim***.
27. Philip (Australian) and Leanora (Peruvian) aboard ***Pompero II.***
28. Dave (English) and Elki (German) aboard yacht ***Strawberry Dragon***
29. Eric and Rosilyn (British) aboard WIGGY.
30. ***Mermaid*** anchored at Tahuata Island in the Marquesas Islands.
31. Paul Gauguin, buried at Hiva Oa, a painter of Polynesia in the 1800's.
32. A tropic bird caught in the cockpit.
33. A booby catching a lift as we passed Booby Island, Australia.
34. A crocodile's tail power.
35. Marione sitting on a true scale replica of the largest saltwater crocodile caught in the Northern Territory, Australia.
36. A small termite hill on the Barrier Reef of Australia.
37. A Hindu temple in Mauritius.
38. The Coelacanth fish thought extinct and discovered alive in 1932.
39. Marione dressing like the natives in Mauritius.
40. Women in Malagasy heading home from market.

41. The kids that wanted a picture more than money in Malagasy.
42. Marione and I at Kuranda, Australia.
43. Marione showing a natural beauty.
44. The Barrier Reef on the east side of Mayotte.
45. The mountains around Hout Bay, South Africa.
46. 100 miles south of St. Helena Island in the South Atlantic.
47. The town of Jamestown on St. Helena Island in the South Atlantic.

March 29: The wind was south southeast at ten knots. Our course was 247 degrees true. We moved southward in order to pick up the stronger trade wind and the Humboldt Current, which moves to the west in this part of the Pacific.

March 30: The wind was five knots and we had an eight-foot south ocean swell creating a sail-slapping situation. Our position was 06 degrees 24 minutes south and 91 degrees 18 minutes west. Our course was 250 degrees true. Later, the wind picked up to ten knots from the southeast. Still later, I believe we crossed a current. There was a froth line with garbage in it, and a pair of sea turtles playing and relaxing. However, I could not notice much change in the water temperature. A lone frigate bird was gliding and soaring, and a brown booby flew by, then a number of terns.

March 31: The wind was east southeast and light during the night, but picked up during the day.

April 1: We had a steady wind from east southeast at twelve to fifteen knots. The waves were east southeast at five feet with a south swell to nine feet. Our course was 262 degrees true, and our position was 06 degrees 55 minutes south and 94 degrees 54 minutes west.

April 2 through 11: The wind held true and steady, easterly at fifteen to twenty knots.

April 12: The wind decreased to five to eight knots with three-foot waves and we had scattered showers. The wind shifted from east southeast to east northeast then three hours later, it shifted back to east southeast at fifteen to twenty knots. Our position was 08 degrees 50 minutes south and 115 degrees 10 minutes west.

April 13: The wind was east southeast at fifteen knots and variable with occasional showers.

April 14 through 19: The wind remained steady, east southeast, at five to twelve knots. On the 19th, our position was 10 degrees 29 minutes south and 125 degrees 04 minutes west. That day, we sighted thirteen birds flocking and feeding.

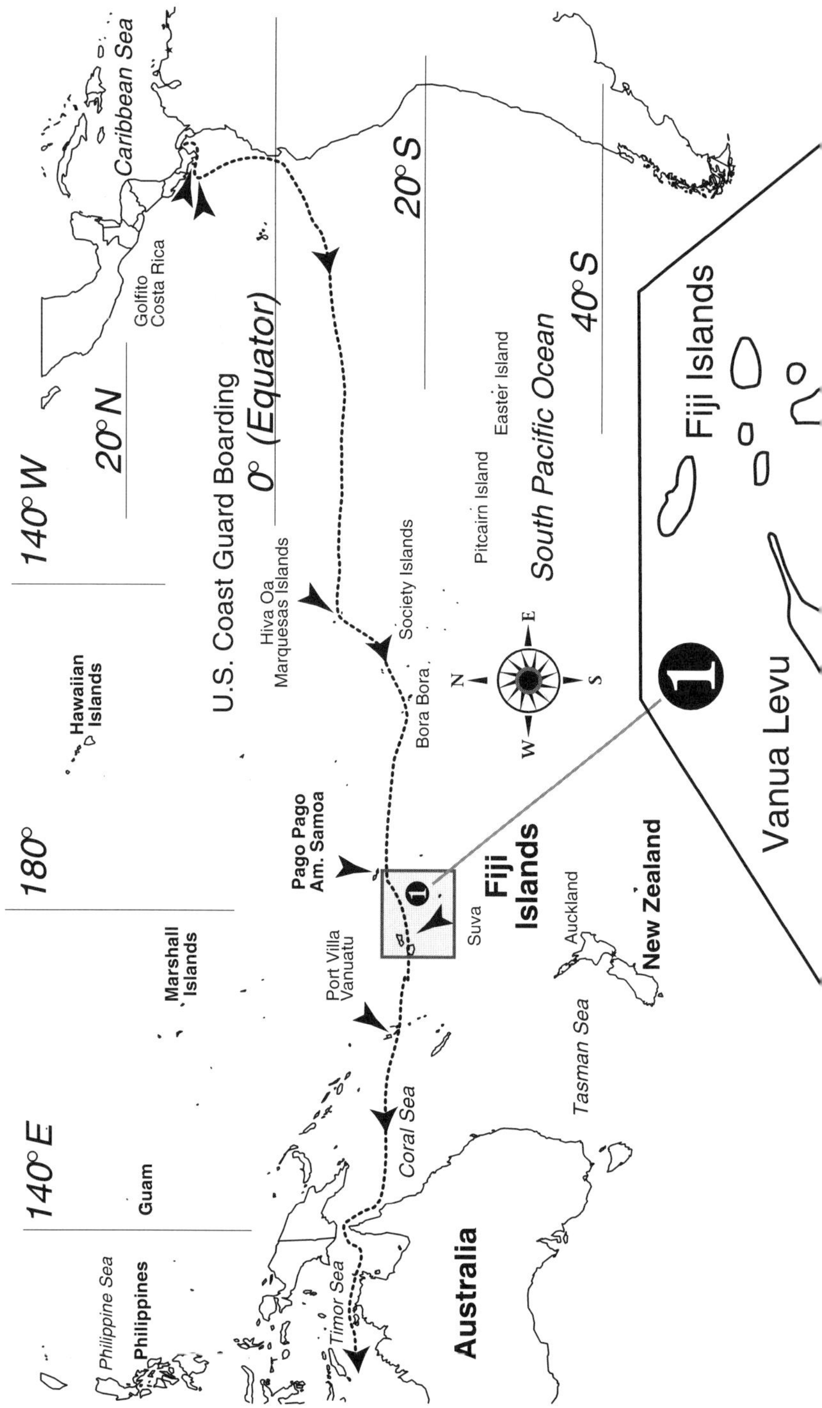

Caribbean Sea
Golfito
Costa Rica
20° N
20° S
40° S
0° (Equator)
140° W
180°
140° E
U.S. Coast Guard Boarding
Hawaiian Islands
Hiva Oa
Marquesas Islands
Society Islands
Bora Bora
Pitcairn Island
Easter Island
South Pacific Ocean
N
E
S
W
Pago Pago
Am. Samoa
Marshall Islands
Port Villa
Vanuatu
Suva
Fiji Islands
Auckland
New Zealand
Tasman Sea
Coral Sea
Guam
Philippine Sea
Philippines
Timor Sea
Australia
Fiji Islands
Vanua Levu
1

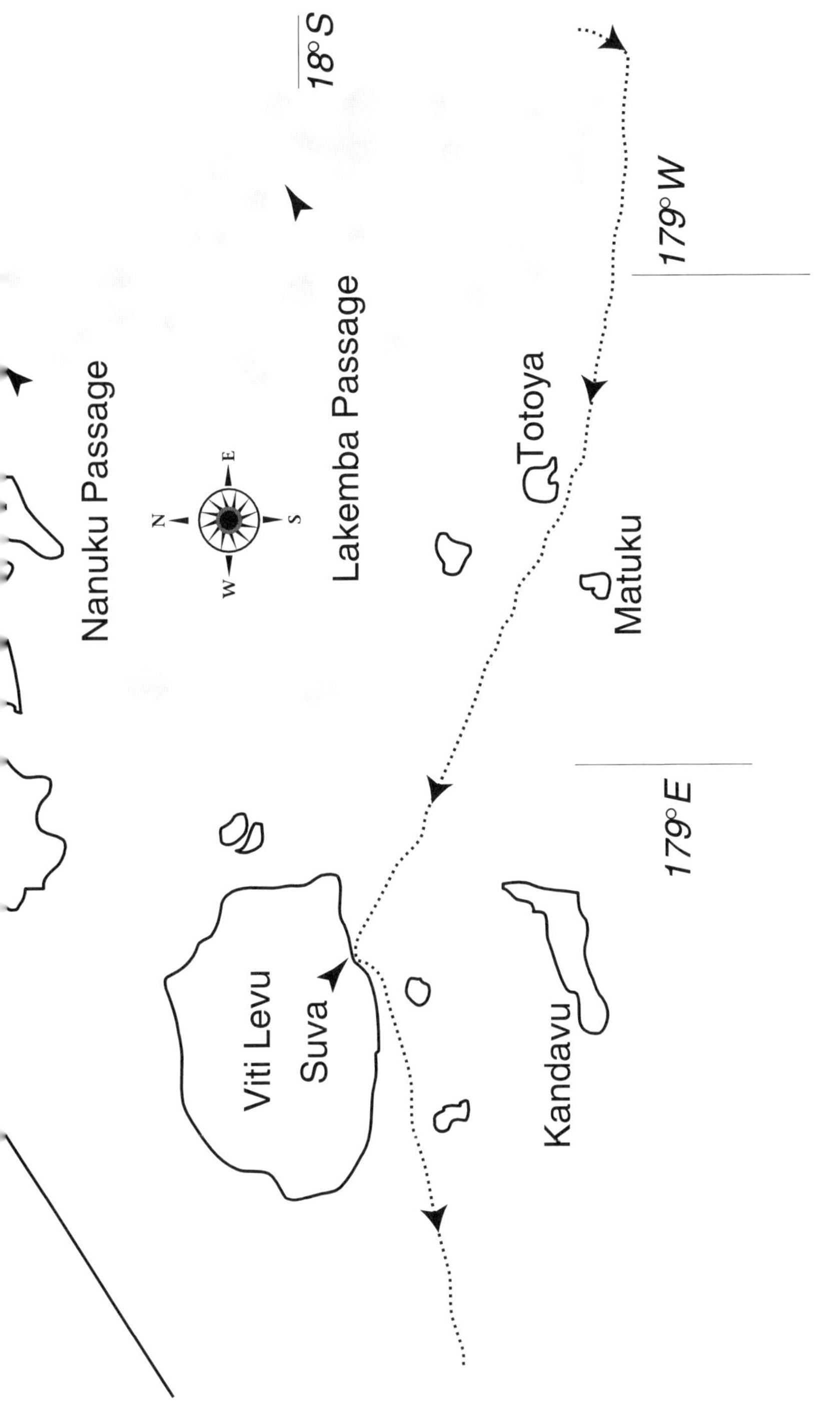
18° S
179° W
Nanuku Passage
Lakemba Passage
Totoya
Matuku
N
E
S
W
179° E
Viti Levu
Suva
Kandavu

April 20 through 25: The wind was light, five to eight knots, and variable. The waves were larger than the wind warranted, consequently, we had slapping sails with the south swell. To end the sail-slapping, I motor-sailed through this area with a fuel-efficient 1200 RPM.

April 26: There was a full moon in the west and rain showers in the east, and with this combination we saw our very first ***moon-rainbow.*** It was a full arch and very bright, but the only color displayed was a bright red at the top of the arch. The rest was white. The wind returned from the east at fifteen knots. Our course was 268 degrees true and our position was 09 degrees 02 minutes south and 134 degrees 11 minutes west.

April 27 and 28: There was a clear sky. The wind was east southeast at fifteen knots. There was a three-foot wave from the southeast. By this time, ***Mermaid's*** bottom was covered with gooseneck barnacles, even though the bottom paint was less than six months old.

MARQUESAS ISLANDS

April 29,1991: We sighted Mohotani and Hiva Oa in the Marquesas Islands, a French possession. In the afternoon, we anchored at Atuona on the island of Hiva Oa, alongside some thirty other boats. Most of them were participating in the Jimmy Cornell Around the World Cruising Race.

As stated previously, before leaving Panama, we had picked up a visa for Marione at the French Consulate. Our plans had been to stay in French Polynesia for only thirty days. The Pacific is big and we wanted to be in Australia before the hurricane season started in December. I had inquired at the consulate in Panama as to whether we had to post a bond for a thirty-day stay. The official there told me that it wasn't necessary.

Upon our arrival at Hiva Oa, we proceeded to check in for our thirty-day stay. We were informed that we'd have to post a bond with enough money for an airplane ticket for each of us to return to our home countries! That wasn't enough! In posting the bond, I'd have to pay the bank a fee to accept my money! The bank could then use my money, ***interest-free,*** for the duration of our stay. I would also have to make arrangements to pick up my money when we decided to clear out. I must say that I don't care if the Garden of Eden is there! I don't pay a bank to take my money! What's more, no bank gets my money without paying interest. So, I told this run-down, worn-out immigration man, who had obviously dealt with too many yachtsmen in his day and didn't like his job, that I was not putting down any deposit. He gave us a seven-day permit. He cared even less about Marione's visa. We decided then and there that there would be no more applying for visas in advance for small countries. If a country would not issue a visa when we arrived, we would sail right on out of there.

Those planning on a longer stay in French Polynesia, who also find paying a bank to keep your money without interest as annoying as I do, may want to follow the strategy of a fellow yachtsman we met there. Life was very easy for him because he had bought a one-way airline ticket from Tahiti to Hawaii beforehand. Consequently, he didn't have to mess with posting bonds. He simply showed immigration his ticket out, and was cleared in without hassle. He planned to get his refund from the airline after he left French Polynesia. Granted, when you follow this plan, the airline has your money interest-free. But you don't have to pay them to take it.

While we were there, an Australian boat cleared in without having to post a bond. I don't know if that is the case for all Australian boats. Another yachtsman borrowed time by telling immigration that he was waiting for money to be wired to him there.

These islands are rocks jutting out of the ocean with mostly scrub foliage. But, in the valleys, the soil is rich. Many trees bear edible fruit. Usually, there are clouds obscuring the mountain tops in the afternoon. Visibility can be great when closing or leaving the islands, as we experienced when leaving Tahuata, an island ten miles southwest of Hiva Oa. We could see the islands to the north. The closest was Ua Pou, some sixty-five nautical miles away. Earlier, however, as we closed Hiva Oa, it was hazy with about ten miles of visibility.

We enjoyed our walk around the bay to town. Along the road, there are many fruit trees and flowers. Everyone coming by in a car offered us a lift. So, it was hard to get exercise without turning down many rides, but nice to meet so many friendly people.

We walked up to the cemetery and took a look at Paul Gauguin's grave. Although he died in 1903, there were still fresh flowers on the stone. He was a man who sailed to the South Pacific in the eighteen hundreds and who became a famous painter of Polynesia.

After looking around, we felt a week was long enough here. The anchorage was crowded. A small surge comes into the harbor and makes the boat roll. What's more, prices were high. A medium t-shirt was $28.00 U.S. The exchange rate was 102.25 Polynesian francs to $1.00 U.S. Surprisingly, diesel fuel, which came from a small freighter, was only $2.05 U.S. per gallon, about the best buy there.

SAILING THE CONVERGENT ZONE

May 7, 1991: We cleared out of Hiva Oa, planning to sail to Bora Bora to clear back in for the rest of our thirty days. But first, we wanted some clean water to scrub the gooseneck barnacles off the bottom of ***Mermaid***. So, we sailed into Tahuata Island ten miles from Hiva Oa. We anchored alone in another light surging anchorage. The mountains were a lovely green and the water was nice and blue. We scraped the bottom and weighed anchor for Bora Bora. The wind was east southeast at ten to fifteen knots.

May 8: The wind dropped to three knots, shifting from southeast to northeast, and we motored all night.

May 9: There was a clear sky and a five-knot wind. We motor-sailed in small swells from the northeast and southeast, overlapping. Birds and fish ran with us all day.

May 10: The wind came in from the north at twelve knots. The wind shifted to the northwest and then west northwest at seven knots. Our position was 12 degrees 10 minutes south and 143 degrees 47 minutes west.

May 11: The wind was light from north northwest. There were thundershowers in the evening.

May 12: The wind picked up at sunrise from the north northwest at fifteen knots. Our course was 241 degrees true with a west swell from five to eight feet. Waves were three to five feet from the north northwest. Later, the wind dropped and became variable in all directions.

May 13: The wind was northwest to west northwest at twelve knots. Later, it shifted directions and the speed became variable.

May 14: There was a light wind at five knots, shifting west. There were squalls and showers all around us. Our position was 14 degrees 47 minutes south and 148 degrees 59 minutes west. ***Where was the trade wind?*** The explorers, not knowing where land was, must have had great frustration sailing in this area. There are many mirages with clouds on the horizon that look just like land.

May 15: There were showers and wind squalls to thirty-five knots. Later, it cleared with the wind from the west north-west at twenty knots.

May 16: There was a wind from the west northwest at fifteen to twenty knots. Rain squalls and calm alternated. Later, we sighted Huahine Island near Bora Bora. Then, there was a wind shift to the southwest. We were so happy to see a favoring steady wind that rather than stopping at Bora Bora, we took the port tack and headed for Pago Pago, American Samoa.

May 17: Our course was 280 degrees true, as we sailed on a broad reach. We had fifteen-foot swells with five- to seven-foot waves. The wind was from south southwest shifting to south southeast. Our position was 15 degrees 23 minutes south and 152 degrees 33 minutes west.

May 18: The wind was southeast at twenty knots. The swell was south southeast at sixteen feet. The waves were five to seven feet southeast.

May 19: The wind shifted to east northeast at fifteen knots.

May 20, 21: The wind was east northeast. We had good sailing at night. Showers caused the wind to drop during the day.

May 22: The wind was from the northeast and variable at five to eight knots. We had showers and later the sky cleared. Our position was 14 degrees 10 minutes south and 160 degrees 28 minutes west.

May 23: The wind was southeast to northeast at five to ten knots. Across the South Pacific at 0400 UTC (Universal Time Coordinated) or GMT (Greenwich Mean Time), we received a very worthwhile professional weather report from Arnold's net on 14318 Mhz in the 20-meter band. From it, we learned that, apparently, the wind patterns and sea conditions had changed due to an unusual warming of the ocean. This is known as the El Nino effect. Consequently, the convergent zone was further south than it had been expected to be at this time. The convergent zone, also called the Intertropical Convergence Zone (ITCZ), originates in the semipermanent high pressure belts of the North and South Pacific Ocean. Weather patterns from these belts converge along the equatorial low pressure trough. They meet along the convergent zone, which migrates north and south with the sun.

In the zone, there is high humidity, heavy rains, thunderstorms, and no wind to gusty wind. The zone is responsible for forming up the tropical cyclones (hurricanes) that roam the water west of the 140 degree west longitude in the South Pacific, and all such storms in the North Pacific Ocean during the hurricane seasons.

Our pilot charts, drawn up for normal weather conditions, showed a nice trade-wind pattern for that time of year in the region we were sailing. However, the conditions we were traveling through were far from a nice trade wind! As for pilot charts, in all other areas that I have sailed, I have found that they predicted the conditions very closely. Of course, there are always variables to the projections, but nothing like we were experiencing in this passage.

May 24: The convergent zone was just to our north. The wind was southeast at fifteen knots. Our course was 268 degrees true. During the night, it seemed that the zone crossed through us, moving to the south, bringing rain and more irregular wind patterns. The wind shifted to northeast, to north, to northeast, to east. The rain was heavy and the wind was strong to light. The swell was from the south at twelve feet, with the waves northeast at five feet with a cross swell from the north. It became a very unorganized sea with no wind and slapping sails.

May 25: The morning was calm and the sea had flattened. There was a swell from the south at ten feet and the wind was southeast at seven knots, later increasing to ten knots. Our position was 14 degrees 21 minutes south and 164 degrees 01 minute west. Still later, the wind picked up to fifteen to twenty knots from the southeast with waves from the southeast at seven feet and the swell was southeast at sixteen feet.

May 26: The wind shifted to the northeast and came in with forty-knot gusts and heavy rain. It remained steady at thirty knots for four hours, then shifted north, then northwest to west, and continued to southwest and then to south. Then it quit with the sky clearing, leaving again a very lumpy sea. Our position was 14 degrees 31 minutes south and 165 degrees 52 minutes west.

May 27: The wind was shifting southeast to northeast with passing rain squalls and a fifteen to twenty-knot wind, gusting to twenty-five knots. Later, it shifted northeast to northwest with a clearing sky.

May 28: The wind was south at ten knots and then quit. Later, it picked up again to seven knots from the northeast with a south swell at eight feet. Our position was 13 degrees 58 minutes south and 168 degrees 12 minutes west.

May 29: The wind was variable and light, and the waves calm. So, I decided to start the engine so we could motor. There was a beautiful full moon as we passed by Manua Island, moving toward Pago Pago.

AMERICAN SAMOA

May 30, 1991: We arrived at Pago Pago at 1600 LT and anchored in the bay rather than clearing in, since the clearance offices were closing. Here one clears in at the customs dock and then picks up a buoy. Some buoys have been ***"claimed"*** by some individuals who want to charge rent for their use. However, the port captain told us that no one has the right to own buoys in the harbor but him. His charge is $25.00 U.S. per month in the harbor, whether on a buoy or not. So, a sailor should just pick up a buoy. The port captain is charging you for it. If anybody tries to collect rent, refer him to the port captain.

When we arrived, about thirty boats were there. A good number of them were working toward building up a cruising kitty. American Samoa seems to be a good place to build such a kitty. After a year, one gets free medical treatment.

Starkist and Chicken of the Sea both have canning factories here. A fleet of Albacore long liners and trawlers support the canning factories. The town is small and convenient for provisioning, as well as for obtaining any supplies one might want from the United States. Most provisions are from stateside. Expect good quality at reasonable prices, even for beef. There is a good video store, making it possible to catch up on movies, as well as a nice bowling alley.

This is a harbor of rainbows. Hills flank the harbor on both sides. When the sun is in the west, and the afternoon showers are moving from the east down the harbor, we would see a rainbow arch from hill to hill, and then move right down the harbor. It was a lovely sight in that lush, green setting.

Even though Samoa is an American possession, the U.S. auto industry is apparently not aware of it. It is difficult to find an American car. The Japanese have captured the car business here and the bus business, too. They have a specially-built, smaller car carrier ship to do business with the smaller markets in the islands, such as these. Obviously, they give good service here.

Although the island gets a sizable subsidy from Uncle Sam, the government operates in the red. One newspaper editorial commented that just as soon as the government can send one person to do one person's job, rather than sending seven people to do that one person's job, they might get the budget under control. There are problems everywhere, even in paradise!

Overall, American Samoa is a good stop. We noted just two drawbacks there. First, many people use the creeks as trash disposals. After a heavy rain, the harbor looks like a floating garbage waste disposal with plastic bags and cans everywhere. Second, the diesel generators and the canning plants make quite a bit of noise in the harbor.

Dave and Elki arrived just before we left. We had a good chat. They had heard a most distressing rumor: Eric and Rosilyn had lost their boat at Pitcairn. All of us sincerely hoped this was not true.

July 10, 1991: ***We cleared Pago Pago at a cost*** of $50.00 U.S. for clearance out plus the harbor fee. We were en route to Suva, Fiji Islands. The wind was southeast at twenty-five knots and the waves were southeast at eight to twelve feet. It was lively at the entrance to the harbor, but we pushed through it, knowing that we could turn around and sail back into the harbor if we experienced engine failure.

July 11: There was a southeast wind blowing at twenty knots and the sky was clear to overcast. The convergent zone was over Pago Pago.

July 12: The wind shifted to the northeast at fifteen to twenty knots. We had a seven-tenths cloud cover. Later, the wind shifted to southeast at fifteen to twenty knots. The waves were five feet and the swell was seven feet. Fine sailing! Our position was 16 degrees 35 minutes south and 173 degrees 07 minutes west. A school of dolphins ran with us. I had never seen dolphins with so many injuries as in this region. They all had scars and broken fins. Indeed, the dolphins in this area were in worse shape than any other place I cruised to in my whole circumnavigation!

July 13: There was little wind and a calming sea so we motored. Later, the wind picked up from the south at twelve knots. Still later, it shifted south southwest at fifteen knots with a clear sky. The temperature was 75 degrees F.

July 14: The wind was south southwest at ten to fifteen knots. Thc swcll was south at scvcn fcct. Our plans to close Fiji were to round the south end of the Nuku Song Reef. There is a narrow channel more to the north. However, even though it was clear at the time, I could envision closing that narrow channel under an overcast sky so that I could not obtain a celestial position. Having no shelf before the reef, the depths would be too deep for sounding. In addition, there would be the possibility of wind and sea pushing ***Mermaid*** onto the reef, a situation that I would not like to be in. So, we continued to the south end of the reef where there is plenty of sea room.

July 15: The wind was southeast at fifteen to twenty knots. The waves were five to eight feet. There were scattered clouds. Our position was 18 degrees 34 minutes south and 176 degrees 30 minutes west. A tropic bird had slept in the cockpit during the night. It couldn't get out in the morning because of the many obstructions for its wings. So, I just reached down and picked up this ***wild*** bird. It allowed me to handle it without a problem. I set it down where it could fly and off it went.

July 16: The wind picked up to a steady twenty-five to thirty knots from the southeast. The waves were five to nine feet from the southeast and there was an eighteen-foot ocean swell from the south. It was overcast with showers. Fifty dolphins ran with us today. Later, as we were sailing along with two reefs in the main and the small jib (150 square foot jib) forward, seeming all alone in the ocean, a huge sei whale, larger than ***Mermaid***, shot out of the water just fifty meters off our starboard bow. Its leap climaxed with its back to the water in a horizontal level clearance, about two meters above the water, before it dropped back into the water. It happened so quickly that we asked each other, *"Did that really happen?!"* It did and it was fantastic!

Our position was 19 degrees 44 minutes south and 177 degrees 39 minutes west. This position was obtained with just three quick shots of the sun at thirty-minute intervals, just before and after high noon. That was the only time we saw the sun that day. It was a critical time, as we were plotting our course to go south of the Nuku Song Reef and north of Vanoa Island where there is a fifteen-mile opening.

You can believe that with the wind, those waves, that overcast sky, and rain, I was thankful that we hadn't elected to take the narrow channel to the north. When navigating by celestial, it is necessary to allow greater tolerances than when navigating with electronic equipment. This day most certainly proved that principle for us. Getting those sun lines close to high noon allowed thirty-minute intervals between shots to determine our position. The line of position azimuth (bearing) changes so quickly around noon that, when advancing your lines of position, it is possible to get a nice triangulation. At any other time of day, it might have been possible to get only two lines of position with less angle of intersection with a resulting marginal position, having only one and a half hours between advancing lines.

So by sheer luck of timing, the sun showed itself and I was able to get a good three-line position. With that good position, we were able to sail between the reef and the island in the middle of the cut at 0200 LT on **July 17**, even though we couldn't see anything at all in the poor visibility.

FIJI ISLANDS

July 18, 1991: The wind was blowing twenty-five to thirty knots. It was overcast with heavy rain. We were running our DR (dead reckoning course) to Matuku and Totoya Island. Visibility: none! Running our dead reckoning course to Totoya Island, we heaved to until I could get a position, or until we sighted Totoya Island. Marione and I had a nice sleep while listening to Suva (Fiji) radio, which played pleasant music. About two hours before sunset, the rain stopped and visibility temporarily improved. This is what makes celestial navigating so satisfying: there was Totoya Island, about two miles away. We sailed by it before dark, giving us a position to take a heading toward Suva.

On this leg from Totoya to Suva, 110 miles distant, we crossed the 180 degree longitude line. Thus, we passed from west to east. This is the International Date Line, more or less, depending on how countries bend it to their needs. For me, it made no difference. I set my watch to GMT or UTC, if you prefer, whichever way you think of the zero-degree meridian line. Then I simply add or subtract time zones to establish the local times and dates wherever I may be. Navigating with GMT on your watch saves one step when figuring sights, which is very important when you're tired.

As we passed Totoya Island, we changed course to Suva. Since there was so much rain, I took a direction-finding bearing on the radio station we were listening to. I got the same bearing to Suva that I had calculated for our course from Totoya Island. I took that to mean that the station was in Suva or directly behind it on the course I needed to sail. This gave me an additional reference, since we had a radio signal to track (steering a course that keeps the radio bearing constant) the same bearing to Suva, in addition to our dead reckoning (DR) course. That night, as we ran our DR, we could see the loom of lights from Suva reflecting off the clouds ahead, another reference to assist the navigator in showers and overcast conditions, such as we were experiencing that evening.

July 19: As we were closing the buoyed channel of Suva, a rain squall came off the mountains to obscure the channel. We couldn't see the next buoy. Since this was a channel unfamiliar to us, with reefs on both sides, we turned around and moved out the mouth until visibility improved. When it did, we went back into the channel, entered the harbor, and anchored by the quarantine buoy. As a rule, ***I don't pick up a buoy*** when there is a choice. I sleep much better with my anchor down since I know what is holding ***Mermaid***.

In point of fact, while anchored at Suva, we could see the quarantine buoy. We watched many boats tie to it. One day, a tug left a barge tied to the buoy. A small sou'wester came in blowing at about twenty-five knots. As we watched it, both buoy and barge drifted ashore.

During the same storm, we watched a boat drag by us with its Bruce anchor. We threw a line to the dragging boat and secured it off our stern. Later on inspection, it was discovered that a round rock had gotten caught in the flukes of the anchor so that it couldn't dig into the bottom. I'd seen that happen before with a Bruce anchor.

The morning after our arrival, we went to the main pier to clear in. We cleared in quickly, even without a visa on Marione's Brazilian passport. As I spoke to the immigration man, I showed him a couple credit cards and assured him that we hadn't come there to work. He issued a visa for Marione the following morning.

We enjoyed Suva. It has a good anchorage, though open to the southwest. The port is very pretty and has quite a bit of rain. The island is lush green with jagged mountains covered with stratus clouds that drift into the valleys with misting showers and often heavy rains.

The yacht club was our first stop. It was a good place to leave our dinghy. The charge was $80.00 Fiji per month. The exchange rate was $1.00 U.S. to $1.41 Fiji. There was a better exchange for travelers checks: $1.00 U.S. to $1.44 Fiji. Movies were $1.50 Fiji, ground beef, $1.80 Fiji per kilo (2.2 pounds), a nice medium-sized pizza, $5.50 Fiji; grapes, $1.25 Fiji per kilo, and a new, two-horsepower Yamaha outboard, $470.00 Fiji (or $330.00 U.S.).

There is a very interesting museum here that describes the history of Fiji. Through its exhibits, it is possible to follow the island's history to the present day. This was the first cannibal museum I had ever seen. As recently as the 1830's, the Micronesians were cannibals. One tribe would war with another for meat. Yet, when prisoners were scarce, and the clan was hungry, they would find someone in their own group who excelled at neither work nor battle. He or she would be dinner. This had to have given everybody an incentive not to be lazy!

Each hunter kept a stone pebble for each person he killed. The most notorious cannibal on the island had 872 stone pebbles. No doubt, he suffered from high cholesterol. War clubs were the main weapons. I wasn't at all surprised to learn a club shaped like a big baseball bat was one of the most effective. It had seventeen notches on it, signifying seventeen victims.

The Micronesian people are physically big. They would have been most intimidating and formidable charging at a person, or waiting on the beach while a small boat was making landfall-especially with their huge Afro haircuts! Sometimes, their hair measured a meter across, that being the style at the time.

The museum also has a good selection of catamarans on display. This was the first time I had seen a replica of an original Micronesian catamaran. It was interesting to me that when going to windward, rather than tacking across the wind, the Micronesians would simply shift the mast from the forward position to the aft position and sail off in the other direction. Hence, the stern of the boat became the bow of the boat.

Through accidentally-introduced diseases, the native population dropped from eighty thousand to twenty thousand. Then the British brought in Indian serfs from India to work the sugar plantations. Consequently, the population today consists mainly of Micronesians and Indians. There is also an Asian group, as well as an English one.

There is a good library here as well. I got my hands on an old, thick book containing the log records of the three voyages of Captain James Cook. They were to add to my enjoyment along this leg of our journey, especially along the Australian Great Barrier Reef.

I took time out in Suva to rerig Mermaid. I had been seeing breaks from rust in many strands of her cables. I bought a reel of 7-19 stainless cable with the agreement that the store would buy back what was left over at the same price I had purchased it at. ***Mermaid*** has steps on her mast. So, it's simply a matter of taking one stay or shroud off at a time, rebuilding it on the deck, and putting it back. I use double sleeves and thimbles on my rigging. There are a few good reasons for doing this. The cost is less than with other systems. ***They are easy to inspect.*** I can swage (press the sleeve tight to the cable) them on the boat, making repairs easy.

I use a three-quarter inch, steel plate, a big, coal chisel with the cutting edge blunted flat, and a hammer for a swage-it tool, to press the double sleeves to the cable. It is a simple matter of laying the double sleeve on the steel, fitting it tight to the thimble with the cable, and hammering on the blunted, coal chisel on the double sleeve between the two cables, pressing the double sleeve to the cables. Don't bury the chisel in so deep that you crack the side of the sleeve that is between the chisel and the cables. This procedure can easily be done with a five-sixteenths cable. I put three double sleeves on each cable end, leaving a tailing up a bit to mark it. Then, when I check it, I can determine whether the cable is slipping. I have never had a cable slip, and have experienced wind to seventy knots at sea.

The cost of my re-rigging was $1000.00 U.S. This included two mainstays, two top shrouds, two running backstays, four lower shrouds, two wisker stays, and a bobstay. All of these were five-sixteenths stainless cable with three double sleeves on each end of each cable, and thimbles for a forty-two-foot mast.

Suva, Fiji Islands is a great mecca for cruising boats. There are many yachts coming and going. However, the anchorage is big. We never felt crowded. Fiji is on the north end of a yearly cruising circuit for many yachtsmen who prefer to stay in the Pacific. Their winters are spent in the Fiji Islands or surrounding island groups. They summer or wait out the hurricane season in New Zealand. For cruisers who want to spend a few years in the Pacific, it's a good route to take.

Fiji has sea snakes about the same size as those in Panama. In Fiji, they are white with black spots while in Panama, they are green with red spots. Both species are about two feet long.

While washing ***Mermaid's*** waterline from the dinghy one day, I saw a sea snake swimming around the boat at the waterline. Every time it came around, I had to remove my hand from the water. It got to be annoying! It just kept swimming around the boat. Finally, I gave it a slap with the oar, and it left. A short time later, a friend stopped over with his rubber dinghy for a chat.

As he began to get back in the dinghy to leave, I said, *"Hold it! There is a sea snake in your dinghy!"*

That snake or one like it, had crawled into the rubber dinghy. We didn't know much about it. So, we opted to kill it rather than trying to pick it up to throw it back into the water. That's when I learned two interesting things about this species of snake. First, it has absolutely no fear. Even while it was being killed, there appeared to be no retaliatory reflex to bite, until after it had taken five or six hits, and was cut in half. Second, it does not have the ability to coil and strike. It seems to be very weak out of the water. However, these snakes are very graceful and fast in the water. Up to that time, I had no idea one might want to come out of the water.

While in Suva we saw a mutual friend who knew Eric and Rosilyn on ***Wiggy.*** To our great sadness, he confirmed that ***Wiggy*** had been lost. ***Wiggy had been anchored in the lee of Pitcairn*** with two other boats. During the night, there was a wind shift, which left them on the windward side with a swell, and gave them a dangerous and unpleasant anchorage. Eric heard a snap and he got up to look around. All looked well, so, he went back below. However, the snap Eric had heard was the anchor chain breaking. Since a boat drifts slowly, when he looked, it appeared that they had not moved at all. The next thing they knew, they were in a big breaker on the shore, with ***Wiggy*** laid over in the breaker. All they could do was climb the mast to get above the breaker and hang on. It was night and the shore was vertical with cliffs. There was no way to leave the boat safely. The two other boats were unaware of what was happening to ***Wiggy***. Finally, Rosilyn couldn't hang on any longer. She fell to the surf and rocks. Eric held on and was able to get off in the daylight. Then he got help from the other boats, but it was too late to save Rosilyn or ***Wiggy***. Such a sad ending for the great adventure they were both having.

We can get to a point where we trust our equipment too much. When it fails, we are caught offguard.

A fisherman friend once remarked, ***"One anchor is like no anchor, and two anchors are like one anchor."***

There's a lot of truth in that! The only way I sleep, even a little in a dangerous anchorage, is with two anchors down, and someone standing anchor watch.

Dave and Elki had gone north of the Fiji Islands, then closed Latuka on the west end, about one hundred miles from us. They came to Suva by bus. We swapped sea stories. It's great fun when friends catch up with each other while cruising. Since everyone is living an adventure, conversation is not dull!

While in Suva, we picked up visas for Australia. Our clearance out cost was nothing. Clearance in was $ 32.00 Fiji.

PORT VILLA, VANUATU

September 13, 1991: We departed Suva in the morning en route to Port Villa, Vanuatu. The sky was clear with a land breeze. By noon, it was overcast. By 1500 LT, it was raining. It rained throughout the night. The wind was southeast, shifting to northeast at fifteen to twenty knots.

September 14: There was heavy rain which changed to light drizzle. The sky remained overcast. The wind shifted northwest. It continued shifting to south during the night. ***Mermaid*** sailed close to the wind through the night.

September 15: The wind was south at fifteen knots and the cloud cover was six tenths. We saw many birds. One flock was jet black and flew very fast. We also saw brown boobies and sea gulls. Our position was 19 degrees 28 minutes south and 175 degrees 50 minutes east.

September 16: The wind was south to southeast at fifteen knots. The waves were southeast at five feet with a swell to eight feet from the south southeast. The sky cleared and we saw the beautiful Southern Cross and Magellan's Clouds, which are both so visible in the southern hemisphere.

September 17: It was a beautiful day. The wind was east to southeast at ten knots. Our position was 18 degrees 14 minutes south and 172 degrees 14 minutes east.

September 18: We had a nice trade wind from the east northeast at ten to fifteen knots.

September 19 and 20: These were beautiful days, but the wind was only five knots. We motor-sailed.

September 21: The wind was only five knots, but it was a very nice day. We arrived in Port Villa, Vanuatu, previously known as the New Hebrides Islands. There were about one hundred yachts. Port Villa was designed for the yachtsman or tourist to have a pleasant place to stay while in the country. There is a yacht club with a restaurant and hot showers. The clearance fee of 63000 Vanuatu francs ($1.00 U.S. bought 106 Vanuato francs) allowed use of these amenities. Clearance in was easy and efficient with customs and immigration coming to the quarantine buoy.

What I found interesting while being cleared in was the immigration man's way of talking in close quarters. He held his hand in front of his mouth. I saw this also in Malagasy later in our travels. I believe it to be the polite way to communicate in close quarters in light of the widespread tuberculosis in these areas. I also noticed that the immigration man had a stretched, lower lip, into which a wood piece could be inserted for tribal affairs. While I was topside with the immigration man, the customs man was below, ready to come up. He told Marione that he loved her and wanted her to stay in Vanuatu with him. Beautiful women are certainly an international language!

The water in the harbor is clear. Most of the anchorage is deep. So, many boats crowded into the shallow area. We anchored near the quarantine buoy where the water is fifty feet deep. It is further from the yacht club, but we had good drag room with protection in a blow. It is also possible to tie to the seawall. Many boats did just that.

CAIRNS, AUSTRALIA

September 27; We departed Port Villa en route to Cairns, Australia in the morning. There was a sunny sky and an east southeast to east northeast trade wind blowing at fifteen to twenty knots. The waves were five to eight feet. Variation was 12 degrees east.

September 28: We were running on a broad reach with east to southeast wind at fifteen knots. There was a thin cirrus overcast.

September 29: There was no wind. So, we motored on a course of 269 degrees true on a flat sea.

September 30: The wind returned from the east northeast at ten knots, then dropped in the evening.

October 1: We had morning wind at five knots from the northeast and variable, picking up in the afternoon from the southeast at fifteen to twenty knots. The sky was nine-tenths overcast.

October 2: It rained most of the day. The wind was ten knots from the southeast. I took a two-line position: 14 degrees 24 minutes south and 161 degrees 17 minutes east. We encountered a patch of very turbulent water which seemed to be boiling. The turbulence was confined to a two-mile circle. I sounded, but found no bottom at one thousand feet.

October 3 through the 8: We had a southeast trade wind at fifteen to twenty knots. The sky was clear and the blue sea sparkled. We saw many fish jumping around. We also saw many birds. There were some black and white birds with forked tails called sooty terns, and also some birds that were black with brown stripes on their wings called shearwaters. Our position on the 18th was 15 degrees zero minutes south and 150 degrees 17 minutes east. The wind began dropping.

October 9: We had calm conditions and then a light south southwest breeze. We motor-sailed. There were many birds, including brown boobies, slender-billed shearwaters, white winged petrels, a black great frigate bird, sooty terns, and a neat, little bird that was brown and white with black trim which is called a Wilson petrel. With its wide wing, the Wilson petrel flies slowly, gliding just above the water. It seldom flaps its wings. Instead, it just pops its foot down to the water and pushes occasionally to gain a little lift and speed to glide on.

Earlier in my travels, while in the North Atlantic, I had seen another bird with a unique way of propelling itself. It was a Fulmer, a real speedster. It is black and white. It gained lift by slapping its wing tip on the water.

October 10: The wind was four knots from the northwest. We motored, and sighted several whales and many birds. The Australian Customs plane buzzed over us. Our position was 16 degrees 06 minutes south and 147 degrees 46 minutes east.

October 11, 1991: It was calm in the morning. The wind picked up in the afternoon to fifteen knots from the southeast. We sighted the Grafton Lighthouse in the afternoon. We closed the channel and went through the Barrier Reef at the Grafton Pass. The Grafton Pass is a good place to go through. There is a high, steel structure easily sighted by day, which provides a good light at night. We continued on to Cairns, Australia.

We chose Cairns as our destination in Australia on the advice of fellow yachtsmen. They told us that the best part of the Barrier Reef is from Cairns on toward the north. Other friends familiar with the area had commented that 1,500 miles of reef is a long sail. Since we tended to agree with them, we decided to anchor at Cairns for the hurricane season and run only the best 500 miles of the reef .

Clearance at Cairns was fast and easy. We had been aware of those items the agriculture inspector was likely to take from us. We had most of these eaten up by the time we arrived. However, he took our honey, our Nido powdered milk, fresh produce and any canned meat not produced in Australia. Our fresh produce was down to one onion. We had no canned meat other than our canned tuna, in which he took no interest. He took a little honey in a container. We had some Anchor powdered milk which is made in New Zealand so it was allowed entry. Unfortunately, I had put some Anchor milk into a small Nido powdered milk can for ease in handling. Since I couldn't prove it was Anchor milk, he took my Nido can as well.

Once cleared at the marina dock at the mouth of the Trinity Inlet, we had the option of going across the inlet to anchor, of paying to tie to the pilings, bow and stern, or to go up the Trinity Inlet from the anchorage into calmer water where we could anchor in the river. We chose to go up the inlet and found Smith Creek branching off. We decided to follow it to the Cairns Cruising Squadron Club. The club offered us its facilities for $20.00 Australian per month. This gave us a wonderful place to leave our dinghy, have hot showers, and enjoy eating in a congenial restaurant.

We anchored in Smith Creek above the club with a few other cruisers and local boats. Surprisingly, most boats stayed down at the mouth or paid for the mooring at the pilings, since that was closer to downtown Cairns. We settled in very nicely. Next, we had to have transportation. I had considered buying a car. But Australia was in the middle of an awful recession. I figured resale wouldn't be so easy. After looking into the alternatives, we decided that the easiest way to get around Cairns was to buy a bike.

We purchased a shiny, new, ten-speed bike with a seat installed on the back for Marione. After all, she weighed only eighty-eight pounds. We kept the bike at the club when we weren't using it. Cairns is flat so getting around there on a bike is easy. There are painted lines for bikes on the roads. It was just like having bike roads in some areas.

We had a ball in Cairns. There is a great library where we caught up on the happenings while we were cruising, and also read a lot of good books. Woolworth's Grocery Store was good for shopping. They delivered to the cruising club at no charge.

We simply took a lovely three-mile bike ride to town to buy what we wanted, and picked it up at the club to put in our dinghy for transport to ***Mermaid***.

With our transportation problems solved, we needed just one more item: a TV. Our American-made TV did not work in Australia. Both picture and voice are on different frequencies than those used in America. So, we purchased a little TV, set it on top of our American TV, and began to learn about Australia. Between visiting the library, and watching television news and the public broadcasting station (PBS), we learned a great deal about the country while in Cairns. We were able to do this in an easy, relaxed way, gaining real insight into the working community that we were visiting.

Prices in Australia were moderate with an exchange rate of $1.00 U.S. to $1.30 Australian. Diesel was $0.63 Australian per liter; bananas, $1.99 Australian per kilo; and oranges, $3.96 Australian per kilo. We were a bit disappointed with the mango prices, about $1.00 Australian for just one mango and that's where they grow! We'd been getting four or five mangoes (mangos) for $0.50 U.S. Since we both love mangoes, we had to find a better supplier.

We had traveled many roads in the residential areas of Cairns and remembered having seen a couple of old houses on one street with big mango trees in the yard and mangoes all over the ground. One day, while coming back from the library, we stopped at one of the houses and knocked on the door. I asked the woman who answered if we might buy some mangoes from her.

She laughed and replied, *"Buy? You can have all you want! We hate them and they are a real nuisance on the ground."*

For the next four months, we helped get the mangoes off the ground and ate mangoes to our hearts' content.

After a couple of months of happily riding our bike double, it became illegal. A law went into effect that bikers could no longer ride double. It also required that bikers wear hard hats while biking. So, our travel arrangements were no longer legal in Australia. Nevertheless, we went on our merry way as tourists, who just didn't know all the big brother regulations in Australia. No one bothered us.

Sometime later, we moved back down Smith Creek and anchored in Trinity Inlet, upriver from the marina pilings. A friend we met there told us that boats had been removed from three rows of the pilings. While dredges had been working in the area, they found an unexploded 250-pound bomb, a remnant of World War II.

We took a fifty-mile train ride to Kuranda in the small Australian rain forest. It was an enjoyable train ride. We had the whole car to ourselves with one other family. We went on an off-market day.

The rain forest is full of large fruit bats, just as Cairns is. Every night at sunset, we saw these bats flying out for the night. They look to be the size of a large crow. We had our first opportunity in Kuranda to see them close up, hanging in the trees. These bats are eaten in some countries. They say they have a very sweet meat. The bats themselves are very fussy eaters. They eat only untouched fruit.

We returned from Kuranda to Cairns that same evening. The next morning, I read in the paper that the Australian Coast Guard had towed in a sailing yacht in distress off the Barrier Reef to the north. Later, we met the fellow at the Cruising Squadron Club. He was Japanese and had single-handed from Japan. He was about seventy years old. His family was encouraging him to stop sailing. But, he was an adventurer. He wasn't ready to quit yet.

While anchored in New Guinea, he had been boarded, beaten, and ***robbed.*** He'd left his boat ***open*** at anchor while he slept. The thieves came aboard at night. After recovering from that unfortunate incident, he sailed for Cairns. ***His G.P.S. quit en route.*** So, he got out his sextant to work some celestial sightings. When his boat rolled, he lost his balance and dropped his sextant overboard.

He knew he was off a big, dangerous reef with strong wind, and seas capable of pushing him onto the reef. Not knowing where he was, he feared closing and finding a reef wall rather than a channel. He could lose his boat, or worse, his life, on the reef. So, he put out a distress call. He was found a hundred miles from Cairns and assisted to Cairns.

Cairns has an organized plan for when a hurricane approaches the area. The information is available at the port captain's office. The overall tactic is for all boats to go into the inlets and tie into the mangroves. The plan is needed since each mooring area is assigned to a different inlet. We were lucky! There were no hurricanes in Cairns that year. The history of hurricane tracks show that Cairns is not likely to be hit by a hurricane often. To the north, hurricanes are even less likely. Thursday Island rarely, if ever, has hurricanes. However, west of Gove, closing Darwin, potential hurricanes are a threat once more.

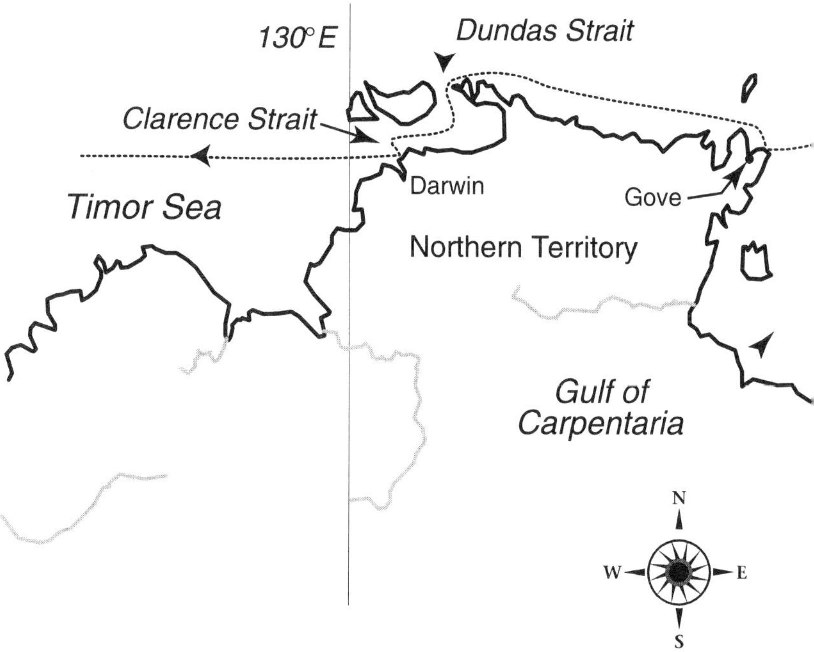
130° E
Dundas Strait
Clarence Strait
Darwin
Gove
Timor Sea
Northern Territory
Gulf of
Carpentaria
N
W
E
S

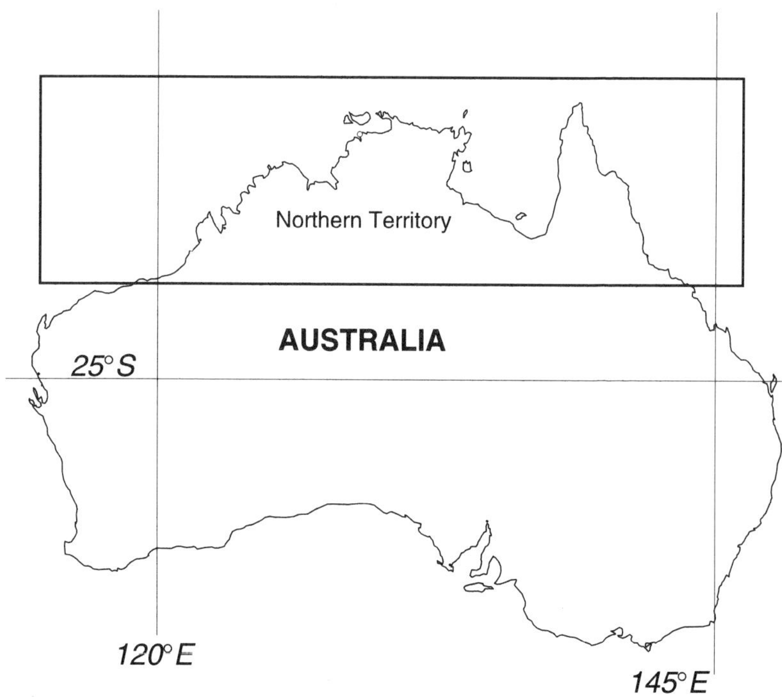
Northern Territory
AUSTRALIA
25° S
120° E
145° E

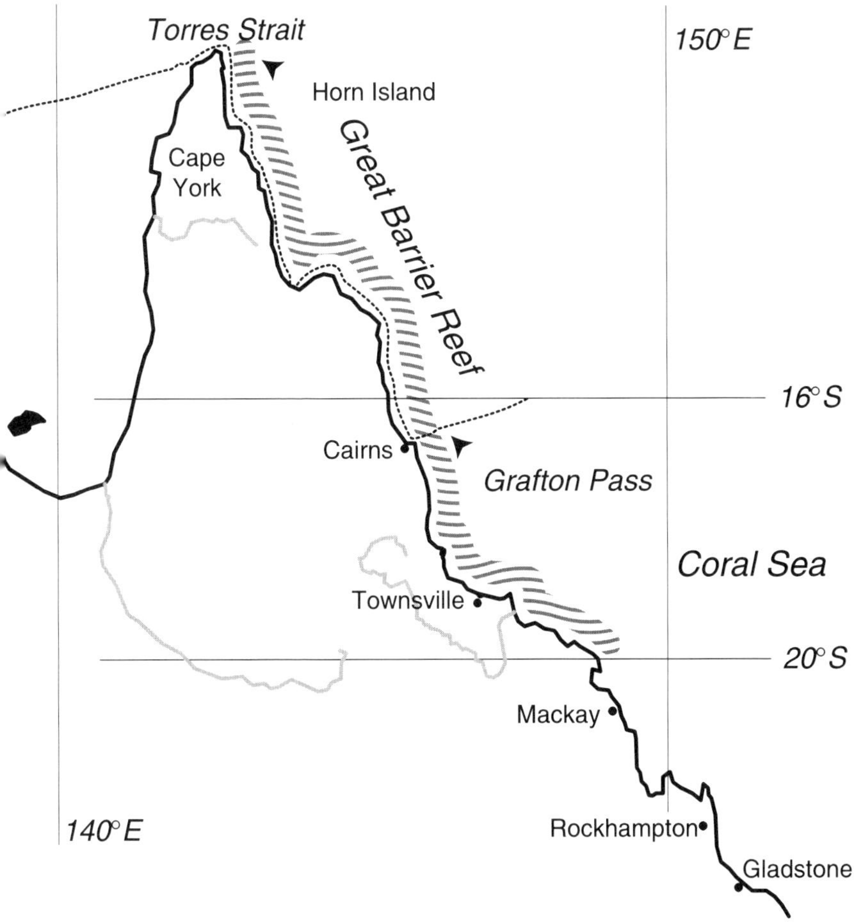
Torres Strait
150° E
Horn Island
Great Barrier Reef
Cape
York
16° S
Cairns
Grafton Pass
Coral Sea
Townsville
20° S
Mackay
140° E
Rockhampton
Gladstone

CRUISING THE GREAT BARRIER REEF

It was March 1992: We were getting ready to cruise the reef. It is required to file a cruising plan before heading up the reef. That way the authorities have an idea of where you are going at all times.

One may ask, *"How can we file a cruise plan when we haven't been there before and don't know where we want to go?"*

Exactly! So, we sat down with an Alan Lucas Cruising Guide for general ideas to make our plan. Then we listed every place we might possibly want to stop. Once the plan is filed, we could stop wherever we chose. While we were there, the government was considering requiring a daily charge for cruising the reef.

About a week before leaving, we moved to the other side of Trinity Inlet, just across from where we had anchored for the previous month. We sold the bike and provisioned for the trip up the Great Barrier Reef and into the Indian Ocean.

March is the last active month of the hurricane season in those parts. It's important to tune your ears to the radio while cruising to be alerted about possible hurricanes, and to have an emergency plan if one should strike. Using the planning guide, we were able to locate four good hurricane holes for safety in riding out a hurricane. They were approximately equal distances apart, up rivers. With this information in hand, and with the low probability of encountering a hurricane here in any case, we were ready to go. We had an almost full waxing moon as planned, and knew we had a well-lighted channel ahead of us. With the moon's light, we had increased our safety if we chose to run the Barrier Reef at night.

The night before we left at around 0220 LT, there was an explosion which shook ***Mermaid*** and impacted her bow. We jumped up and went topside, just in time to see the eighty-foot charter boat, which we had been priorly anchored within 150 feet of, for a month, blown up in its center. It was separating in the middle as if hit by a torpedo. One thing allowed us to stay cool, and that was the knowledge that no one was aboard. The crew that was painting the boat by day went ashore each night. I hate to consider what the impact on ***Mermaid*** might have been had we still been anchored 150 feet from that boat! We were about 150 yards from it, and still really felt the impact. We can thank the mosquitoes for saving us from a very bad impact, since we had moved across the inlet for more wind to get away from them.

We sailed the next morning without learning anything more. We found out later that it wasn't known why it blew up. One theory was that perhaps another unexploded bomb on the bottom had been hit just right by the anchor chain. However, we smelled a great deal of propane after the explosion.

THURSDAY ISLAND AND THE TORRES STRAIT

March 11, 1992: We departed Cairns en route to Thursday Island, proceeding to the north end of Cape York and the Torres Strait. A twelve-knot east southeast breeze was assisting us. We had planned to stop at the low islets, but the going was so good, the channel so well lighted, and the moon so bright that we continued on all night. We passed Endeavor Reef, where Captain James Cook had the unfortunate experience of hitting the reef. Later that same evening, we passed Cooktown where he moved his vessel for careening and for repairs after his unfortunate experience. The only reason the boat had not sunk was that a chunk of coral had plugged the big hole in the bottom.

March 12: The wind was holding as we sailed by Cape Bedford and Cape Flattery. Both are white sand hills and dunes. We anchored on the west side of Cape Flattery at 1800 LT with land and sea breeze conditions, which were mostly light wind.

March 13: We continued north with a light breeze at five knots. The early morning breeze came from the southwest, the afternoon breeze from the northwest. We motored along in a flat sea. That night we anchored in Ninian Bay, just before Cape Melville at 2200 LT.

March 14: Weighing anchor, we leisurely motored by Cape Melville. It is mainly large rocks and boulders with scrub trees. We continued on to the Flinders Group and anchored at Denham Island around 1500 LT. The island is worn rocks with a beige and brown sand beach, mangrove trees, grass, scrub trees, and some larger trees. The water visibility was five feet. However, I dove on a reef and found a rich selection of sea organisms anyway.

We hiked on this island for a couple days and did not see a soul. At this time of the year, most boats are still waiting out the hurricane season and giving the trade wind time to pick up for better sailing. The only boats we sighted were freighters and commercial fishing boats. We never felt crowded by boats of any kind since we seldom saw any.

March 17: We weighed anchor and motored in a calm sea. We anchored again at 2000 LT on the east side of Hannah Island in sixty-four feet of water. We saw a lot of thunderstorm activity onshore with wind favoring the west northwest in the evening.

March 18: We weighed anchor at 0300 LT and motor-sailed north in light air from the northeast. In the afternoon, we saw thunderstorms building onshore. They gave a northwest to west breeze which later shifted to south and then dropped to a calm. We anchored at Cape Direction on the east side, just north of Rocky Islets. There was a three-mile or more stretch of white sand beach on what is usually a windward shore. One bonus we found in sailing when we did was that the trade wind was still down at that time of year. This gave us light air to sail with, or to motor-sail. It enabled us to stop on normally windward shores like this one. That's where the beachcombing is great! On this cape, Captain Cook climbed to the top to look for a passage out of the reefs.

March 19: We beachcombed and swam all day. We collected nautilus shells, a seven-foot oar, two extra five-gallon jugs, some fishnet, fishnet floats, and good rope. We probably could have picked up an additional thirty, five-gallon jugs and two hundred more one-foot diameter fishnet floats. We found none of the now rare glass fishnet floats. Somehow, I am sure there are some of those buried in the sand. Other than the many, mostly bleached and broken, nautilus shells, there was not much shelling. I was surprised at the lack of shell variety.

While hiking, we went over a hill of rock, grass, and scrub trees, where we saw seven-foot high termite hills. Later, when we reached Thursday Island, a native told us that termite hills can get to be twice that high inland. Without a doubt, the castles of Australia belong to the termites!

While going up the reef ***at this time of the year,*** one has to be very careful and observant when swimming because of the box jellyfish. Indeed, the hazard they pose is serious enough that Australians, who use the water a lot, wear jellyfish suits during the season while in the water. These suits cover their bodies completely except for their heads. The sting of the box jellyfish can be deadly. Consequently, it has to be considered deadly at all times.

I am a swimmer. Nevertheless, I was hesitant to swim much on the reef with the box jellyfish, huge sea snakes, saltwater crocodiles, and deadly stone fish. These fish have a nasty habit of digging under mud and sand close to shore. They make wading without hard-soled shoes hazardous. Visibility underwater up the channel is not so great.

Underwater visibility is better in the Torres Strait. However, when we were there, lobstermen were complaining about the low visibility because of so much turbulence in the water. A fisherman friend we met at Thursday Island told us of the day when he had been diving thirty feet down in the water when he saw a crocodile walking on the bottom. Fortunately, it continued away from him which made him feel better.

Besides all of these possible hazards, one must also consider the great white shark. A newspaper story I had just read while in Cairns reported that a group of divers to the south had been diving the reef when a great white shark passed through them, taking one of the divers. His buddy felt the swoosh as the fish went by and saw the large shark with his friend in its mouth as they disappeared out of visual range. What a sad, terrifying experience!

The great white can be anywhere. Indeed, I read an article where a seven-foot great white was caught at Manus, Brazil, one thousand miles up the Amazon River. However, since the great white population seems to be more concentrated in particular areas, especially around South Australia and South Africa, where there are identified breeding grounds, it seems logical that the risk increases when swimming in those waters. From the documentaries and the encounters man has had with great whites, it seems like a losing proposition not to respect them a great deal.

Fortunately, in all my swimming and diving around the world, I've not yet been threatened or had a close call with any sharks. However, I have had encounters with them. One time while I was snorkeling off Indian Key in the Bahamas, a six-foot bull shark swam by. It came in unseen from behind me and passed about six feet from me as it continued to swim out of visual range. Moments later, it swam back so quickly I could hardly see it as it grabbed a fish ten feet in front of me and then quickly swam out of visual range. It became apparent to me that there is little chance of fending off a serious shark attack. A shark doesn't ***necessarily*** give a warning, such as circling, if its going to attack. Generally when I snorkel, Marione rows the dinghy alongside, giving me a place to put speared fish and giving me a quick exit out of the water if I desire. I have never experienced the need to exit quickly, except when I'm cold.

Speaking of sharks, I recall an incident of interest that happened in the Florida Straits. I had heard this story first-hand at a shark-hunter's association meeting in Crystal River, Florida. ***The following story was related*** to the group by the manager of a sea aquarium in Miami. The people at the aquarium wanted to add more sharks to their collection. So their boat was in the Florida straits long-lining for shark. One day, as the boat was returning to the harbor, the captain called the manager to meet them at the dock to see what they had caught. When he arrived, he observed a huge hammerhead shark. Its length was estimated to be over twenty feet. Something had bitten it almost in half on its way to the boat.

I was reluctant to stick my toes in the water along the Barrier Reef. It may have been because I was spoiled by the lovely Caribbean, where a person doesn't have to contend with sea snakes, stone fish, box jellyfish, saltwater crocodiles, or great white shark breeding grounds. The risk of swimming in open water seemed to be so much less in the Caribbean than along the Great Barrier Reef.

March 20: We motor-sailed all day in a five-knot wind on a flat sea under a blue sky. We passed Restoration Island where Captain Bligh saved himself and his men. He made his great sail in a whaleboat accompanied by about seventeen men. The open boat had a freeboard of less than one foot above the water. He crossed the Pacific from Polynesia, avoiding the islands with their forty-foot war canoes and cannibalistic cultures, just to arrive on a dangerous reef with barren islands. He negotiated that reef with the wind and the sea pushing him toward it, finding a channel through, and Restoration Island, one of the few islands with something to eat: coconuts! ***What a man!*** On the evening of the 20th, we anchored at Piper Island.

March 21: We hauled anchor at 0300 LT. We sailed on a nice trade wind all day, passing Cape Grenville which looked like a nice stop. However, when the wind is right, we sail. We passed Sunday Island.

This island is where Bligh stopped to tell a would-be captain, *"We will decide who is captain!"* as he pulled out his sword.

The other man declined and they sailed on to Timor Island, now part of Indonesia. We passed Hannibal and Bushy Islands. We continued sailing all night in this lovely trade wind.

The lights are very good on the Barrier Reef. With a bright moon to assist visibility, it is very easy to run the reef at night. Nevertheless, while coming up the reef, we gained a respect beyond belief for Captain Cook and his crew. Running a one way trip up this reef with its strong southeast wind, with no idea if there is a way out, and no charts has to be the nervous high of a lifetime! What seamen they had to have been, especially the men that took the small boats and ran ahead to find the channel. Our trip up the reef gave us a new perspective on the trials these men went through.

March 22, 1992: We continued sailing all day with an east northeast wind blowing to thirty knots. We closed Cape York at

Albany Light. We moved on to Mount Adolphus. From the charts, it appeared that there would be a good trade wind anchorage in the bay on the west side. But, when we looked it over, we decided that it would not be a good anchorage. There is a strong current on that side. So, we turned and sailed at a fast clip to Thursday Island. When we arrived there, it was immediately obvious that Horn Island, about two miles south southeast of Thursday Island, would provide a better anchorage for the trade-wind condition. We dropped the hook in the lee of Horn Island at 1700 LT.

We spent a lot of time hiking on Horn Island. We had heard there was a gold mine about eight miles up the road past the small, island airport. The mine had been shut down some time previously. So, we decided to walk to the mine to see what was left. As we came over the last hill on the dirt road leading into the mine, we saw the old equipment on the side of the next hill. There were a couple of cyanide tanks, a rock crusher, and a tumbler. The open strip mine was to the side, dug down to about two hundred feet. At the dip of the road in front of us, there was a small creek with a wash to work the river. There was not a soul around.

We walked down to the mine. There, we finally ran into the caretaker who was a pleasure to meet. He showed us around. The miners had originally tunnel-mined in the late 1880's. The tunnel still exists near the strip mine. The caretaker and the manager were in charge of reclamation activities to restore the land back to its original terrain. What a great job they had! Maybe the mine company couldn't make money because of its overhead cost. But the caretaker and the manager could make money. Everywhere we walked, the whole area shone with gold and silver ore. A lot of the ore had fallen off the trucks that were hauling it to the crusher. They picked up all they found, putting it into fifty-five gallon drums for shipment to a processor. They had a fifty-fifty split with the processor on the profits from the ore they picked up.

The ore is rich in gold, silver, and copper. To our casual glance, it appeared to be lying all over the place. The tanks were still full of sediment which had gold mixed in it. The wash down by the river was just the way it had been left when the operation shut down. There was no telling just what was in there. There was not enough gold for a big operation, but there was plenty for a small operator. I suspect it will be a long time before reclamation is completed. I surely hope so. What a waste it would be to bury all that good ore.

One day, we motored our dinghy to Thursday Island. This island has a Micronesian population, rather than an aboriginal population, as on the mainland. Today, the population is small, and one does not feel crowded on the island. It is more expensive here than in Cairns. We didn't plan on buying anything here. In addition, the selection is limited. Otherwise, these islands are fine: tropical, pretty, with lots of palm trees.

While touring Thursday Island, we happened upon an old Japanese cemetery. Thursday Island was once an area where Japanese divers had come in order to collect pearls. There was a sizable Japanese population on the island at one time. Curiously enough, even though this cemetery dated back one hundred years or more, and was no longer being used, someone was maintaining it immaculately. The new local cemetery for the Torres Straiters (the name given to people living by the Torres Straits), which was right next to the other cemetery was very poorly kept up. After World War II, the Japanese and other oriental people then living on the island, as well as in all Australia, were deported, even second generation Orientals.

We enjoyed the Torres Straits with its strong, warm trade wind and blue water. Again, we did not swim for the reasons cited before, and also because of the strong currents. From March to November around Thursday Island and the Torres Straits, the current, with the brisk southeast trade wind, sets west at all times and can be quite strong.

GOVE

April 2, 1992: ***We were ready to head for Gove*** on the west side of the Gulf of Carpentaria. A hurricane was forming in the Arafura Sea, east of Timor. The odds of it coming to Gove were very small, as were the chances that it would come to Thursday Island. Early in the season, a low had formed in the Bay of Carpentaria. It went across Cape York at forty knots. All in all, Gove appeared to be a better hurricane hole than Thursday Island, should a freak storm strike.

We departed Horn Island on a flood tide. We raced by Booby Island with a good current and a southeast wind at fifteen to twenty knots. The sky was hazy and visibility down a bit. Passing Booby Island brought to mind the stories of all the old sailing vessels which passed through and used this island as a mail drop. They would pick up any mail that other vessels had left there. It was a mail service of goodwill which made it possible to deliver seamen's mail east and west. Most fittingly, a brown booby landed on ***Mermaid*** as we passed Booby Island, and rode with us for a few hours as we were running into the shallow Bay of Carpentaria, known for its short choppy sea.

April 3: The wind was east southeast at twenty to twenty-five knots. There were six-foot waves which were vertical and short in spacing. The sky was clear. Later, the wind dropped to eight knots from the southeast with thunderstorms on the north horizon. The waves calmed to a two-foot chop. A sooty tern and a roseate tern rested overnight aboard, leaving in the morning.

April 4: The wind was variable with heavy showers. Most of the time, it was less than five knots. We motor-sailed with sails reefed. Our position was 11 degrees 40 minutes south and 138 degrees 40 minutes east.

April 5: The wind was light and variable. I managed to get one sun line and a radio direction line for determining position. Our whole trip across Carpentaria was an experience of snapshot navigation. Part of the sun would break out for a minute and then disappear. Without proficiency with the sextant, I would have never gotten a shot in such overcast conditions. I managed to determine a position every day, but had to work for it. We entered the boat channel at Gove in a thundershower and anchored at 1900 LT. We took the time for a refreshing clean-up shower in the rain.

Gove offers a good anchorage. There were quite a few Austrailan boats from Perth on their way to go east and south down the reef in the monsoon season, which runs from November 15 to March 15. Those dates include the transition and monsoon season.

A bauxite plant in Gove offers temporary employment from time to time. This creates a good opportunity for boats stopping here to make good money for a cruising kitty. The bauxite plant ships its ore to Richards Bay, South Africa, where they make it into aluminum. While we were in Gove, one of the furnace fireboxes had to be replaced. Some representatives of the plant came to the yacht club looking for temporary laborers. Yachtsmen jump at such an opportunity. They work twelve-hour days until the job is done, making about $1200.00 Australian per week. That will build up a cruising kitty fast!

Gove has a nice yacht club. The bauxite plant provides free bus transportation into town, about ten miles away. The Woolworth store in town offers a nice selection. Prices are a bit higher there than in Cairns or Darwin.

Gove is one place to meet Australian Aborigines. They own the land there. They hang around the yacht club and use the facilities as the yachtsmen do. We met an aborigine family of seven people. The father was chief. Everyone shook hands with us except the chief. My impression was that because of his high status, he didn't shake hands with common people. His daughter told us that he owns the fuel docks and the facilities. When I asked how, she said the facilities had been built on his land. He was paid a usage fee, as well as owning the facilities. Regrettably, it seemed to me that their income was used in a nonproductive way. Those I met seemed to spend their time drinking a lot of beer and were apparently not very concerned about taking showers. Now don't get me wrong, a cold beer on a hot day can be productive, but moderation is the key. These folks lacked moderation, in my opinion.

While in Gove we met a fellow who had ridden out a hurricane at anchor while in the Philippines. ***His fifty-foot trimaran*** was in a protected lagoon with mangrove around it, along with some other yachts. He put down his seventy-five pound Danforth anchor. The anchor held through the whole hurricane. Sadly, the other yachts didn't fare so well. They were down on Plow anchors. The condition was mud with hard bottom a couple of feet down. This hard bottom under the shallow mud prevented the Plow anchors from continuing to dig deeper. The boats with Plow anchors went to the mangroves.

Because the Plow anchor fluke is small, it just plowed through the shallow mud. The Danforth anchor flukes were big enough to have enough resistance to hold in such a bottom condition. Because his anchor held while the others didn't, his trimaran was the only boat to sustain substantial damage, since the other boats hit his on their way to the mangroves.

Another fellow, who used a Danforth anchor told me about the time he had anchored and backed down, setting his anchor to the wind. The bottom was a sticky clay which held the anchor well. When the wind, blowing hard shifted 180 degrees, the anchor broke loose, since the flukes were set the opposite way. It would not reset. The sticky clay on the anchor flukes would not let the flukes pass by the shank to be reset.

On ***Mermaid***, I carry my favorite anchors: a Plow and a Danforth. In combination, they are equal to both of the above problems. In most conditions, either works fine. When in doubt, I put both of them down. There is a one hundred-foot chain and then anchor rope on each anchor.

THROUGH THE WESSEL ISLAND CHAIN

April 20, 1992: We were ready to head for Darwin, Australia, as we wanted to get into the Indian Ocean by June. A decision had to be made about which route to take west. The Wessel Islands are west of Gove. The options are to take a cut through the chain or to go out of our way north of the islands.

One famous cut is called The Hole in the Wall. For safest passage through the hole, one must get to the cut at high slack tide and go through within the first hour of ebbing tide. Arriving later means coping with currents racing through it even faster, almost like shooting rapids. The cut is about one and a half miles long and only one hundred feet wide. This is a questionable allowance should an emergency arise. Both sides of the cut are steep rock, raising the possibility that the wind could be blanked out.

There is another pass through the island chain, called Cumberland Strait, about seven miles north of The Hole in the Wall. I decided to take a look at The Hole in the Wall and see what I thought about going through it. If I didn't like the looks of it, there would be time to get through Cumberland Strait, just to the north, and still make the ebbing tide. The tidal current is significant in this region. The ebb tide flows west so the flood tide flows east through these cuts in the Wessel Island Chain.

We departed Gove at 0900 LT with an east northeast wind at ten knots. Later, the wind dropped. Then it returned with a northeast swell. At 1730 LT, we anchored at Cape Wilberforce, a good anchorage protected by a shore with rock, sand, and trees. The trees were thirty feet high, larger than we had seen in quite a while. We had a beautiful evening with lots of stars.

April 22: We weighed anchor and motor-sailed with light wind to The Hole in the Wall. We arrived at high slack tide. On that day, the hole was approached with a northeast wave setting toward shore. To go through the hole, it is necessary to motor close to the shore to set up for a turn into the hole. Once the turn is made, your option to turn around is limited. If the current is running, there is no turning back. I don't risk ***Mermaid*** for even two minutes if I can help it. Right off, we faced a breaker on a windward shore, just fifty yards away. We'd have to motor down by that breaker on that windward shore a couple hundred yards before the turn into the hole. At that point, there may be no returning. We'd have to depend on our motor and the current for the next mile and a half.

Before committing ***Mermaid***, as a rule of thumb, given a choice, I plan on having at least two out of three options available: sail and motor, sail and anchor, or motor and anchor. Closing and going through The Hole in the Wall offers no sail option and a questionable anchor option. The chart showed no depths. The hole is narrow. I'd have to commit ***Mermaid*** with only one option, the motor. Motors have been known to quit unexpectedly. So, we turned off and went through the Cumberland Strait, which affords all three options.

Later, in Darwin, I heard from a cruiser who had gone through The Hole in the Wall. He experienced a steering failure in the narrows. There were some hair-raising moments until he got the emergency tiller going. He still had the added danger of operating with only one of the three options.

April 23: The wind was east northeast to east southeast at eight knots. Waves were three feet from the northeast. Our position was 19 degrees 46 minutes south and 135 degrees 04 minutes east.

April 24: The wind was fifteen knots from the east. Waves were six feet from the northeast. Going west across this area, we were set south of our course. Our plan was to clear the New Year Island Light to the north. This is necessary in order not to hit land. The light is at the thirty-fathom curve. Running my DR to where I knew the light was, I became concerned because no light was in view. Taking a depth sounding, I found we were in twenty-six fathoms of water. We changed course to a north heading going back to the thirty-fathom curve. We sighted the light about an hour after we had changed course. We had been set a number of miles south of the light. West of the light, there is a low, dark shore ahead.

April 25: We passed the New Year Island Light early in the morning. Then we ran down the twenty-fathom curve, intending to cut through the Dundas Strait. We didn't sight any land, even though the charts indicated we were passing within eight miles. The coastline is low and very hazy. The sky was clear and the wind was ten knots from the east. The waves were three feet. It was a very pleasant sailing day.

DARWIN, AUSTRALIA

April 26, 1992: We sailed through the Dundas Strait three hours before sunrise with good lights and a moon to assist us. After we passed into the Van Diemen Gulf, the wind lightened. We made our turn at Abbot Shoal in the late afternoon. With no wind, we motored toward the Clarence Strait and anchored east of the strait at Cape Hotham at 2200 LT.

When we passed through the Dundas Strait into Van Diemen Gulf, we had a few moments of concern. We started to see what we thought were brown shoaling conditions where the chart said there were none. I believe what I see until I know differently. So, we steered to avoid these apparent shoals. However, more kept showing up until it was impossible to avoid the brown spots. We went right through them with no problems. After a while, we figured out that the tidal currents were spinning up mud from the bottom. The mud was gradually spreading across the bay. It surely looked like shoals!

There can be a fourteen-foot tidal change in these areas. It pays to use currents to your advantage. To do that, I had tide and current information aboard. I had photocopied it at a library in Gove.

April 27: We weighed anchor at 0700 LT in order to catch the last of the ebb tide that flows west through the Clarence Strait. The sky was clear. We had a southeast wind and a nice day. We dropped anchor at the Fanny Bay Yacht Club in Darwin at 1630 LT. With many other boats, we anchored about three-quarters of a mile from the shore because of the fourteen-foot tidal change in the area and the gradual slope of the shore.

The Fanny Bay Yacht Club is great! It offers an honorary thirty-day membership free. The facilities are excellent. The club provides dollies to transport a dinghy to high ground when a person comes ashore at low tide. These can also be used to return a boat to the water at low tide. This is an important service in these parts. There can be as much as about seventy-five yards of shore change, depending on the tide.

Darwin is a most interesting and pleasant city to visit. There is an efficient bus service that enables the tourist to get around easily. There are many interesting things to see. After just a thirty-minute walk from the yacht club, we were walking in fields and trees with many families of wild wallabies, which are members of the kangaroo family. They congregate in groups under the trees. Some of them were chasing and playing with one another. Watching them gave us an appreciation of how efficient they are as travelers in the high grasses and terrain of their natural habitat.

We rented a car one day to drive to the Adelaide River to take a boat ride to see the jumping crocodiles. Over the years, excursion boats have taken short journeys up the river. By hanging chunks of meat tied to strings and poles over the side, they have trained the crocodiles to come vertically out of the water to get the meat. These crocodiles have become very efficient in getting the meat. We watched them come up out of the water with tail power until their back feet were almost clear of the water. This was an important lesson for us in the capabilities of crocodiles and alligators. Be aware if you are in your dinghy! You are not secure if a crocodile wants to come in! Additionally, in the water you would be very lucky to get away from one if it wants you.

On our way back to Darwin, we stopped at a crocodile farm at feeding time. They are fed dead, frozen chickens. The attendant simply beat the chicken on the ground a few times to summon the crocodiles. They sense the sound or vibrations, and they come in. Man and other crocodiles are their only natural enemies. In Australia, man has allowed them to become so abundant, in some opinions, that it has become a real hazard to the human population in some areas.

THE INDIAN OCEAN

Of all the seas I have seen
The one that is the sailor's dream
Is the Indian Ocean
What a wind machine

Day and night
Dark and light
The wind maintains its mighty might.

THE INDIAN OCEAN

We decided to cross the Indian Ocean in June. At this time, the winter trade wind is just beginning to strengthen. Since the Indian Ocean is so windy anyway, we figured it would be a bit more comfortable to transit a little early rather than taking the real blasting trade wind of July and August.

May 18, 1992: We cleared out of Australia and headed for the Indian Ocean. Our wind was southeast in the morning, shifting northeast in the afternoon at fifteen knots. It increased to twenty knots in the evening. We departed on a spring high tide starting to ebb in order to get the best push to the west.

May 19: We had an ideal trade wind condition. The wind was east northeast at fifteen to twenty knots and the waves were three to six feet. Our position was 12 degrees 00 minutes south and 128 degrees 54 minutes east.

May 20: The moon rose and the wind went light for most of the night. We motored for eight hours. The wind picked up in the morning, east southeast shifting to northeast at ten to fifteen knots. We went through some rain showers.

We were buzzed by customs planes twice today. In fact, we had been buzzed by customs planes every day since we had approached within one hundred twenty miles east of Cairns. They continued to buzz over us daily as we sailed up the reef, across the north side of Australia, and now into the Timor Sea. I don't know what they wanted, since I didn't have a VHF capacity, and I didn't care!

May 21: The wind pattern held: east northeast at night, shifting to east southeast in the morning and day from eight to ten knots.

May 22: We had the same wind pattern, but five to seven knots. We had a slow sail, but very pleasant conditions which we enjoyed greatly. Our position was 12 degrees 49 minutes south and 124 degrees 10 minutes east. ***Mermaid*** sailed south of Ashmore Reef. We had seen quite a bit of reef by this time. The sail and moving into the Indian Ocean felt good.

The last Australian Customs encounter came today. A helicopter hovered over us for about five minutes, apparently trying to get a response. I assumed it came off Ashmore Reef. ***Mermaid*** continued moving under autopilot control. I continued reading a good book, unseen under the cockpit awning. The only other place we visited where government surveillance is so oppressive was in the waters off Florida and in the Caribbean where the U.S. Coast Guard boards boats looking for drugs.

May 23: The wind picked up to fifteen knots from the east northeast. We continued to have nice trade wind conditions. We saw many flying fish and dolphins, all with no injuries.

May 24 through 27: We enjoyed a beautiful trade wind. We saw many flying fish, Wilson petrels, brown boobies, and shearwaters. The wind remained at fifteen to twenty knots. The waves and wind came from an easterly direction. Our position on the 27th was 12 degrees 37 minutes south and 114 degrees 59 minute east.

May 28: The wind was calm. We motored on a flat sea en route to Christmas Island.

May 29: The sea remained a flat calm and we continued motoring.

May 30: We motor-sailed in a five-knot wind. There were showers around us. The wind direction was variable, then moved to the southeast at eight knots. The showers came and the wind turned variable once more.

May 31: The wind was variable to calm as we motored in a south swell.

June 1: The wind was slack all night. We picked up in the morning what I believe to be the true Indian Ocean trade wind. There was a twelve-foot swell from the south. The wind was east southeast to east northeast at ten to fifteen knots. Our position was 10 degrees 49 minutes south and 106 degrees 47 minutes east.

June 2 and 3: The wind was east southeast at fifteen knots with a southeast swell of six feet. The cloud cover was a seven-tenths broken condition.

June 3: As we closed the east end of Christmas Island, we saw a new resort being built on the island. We anchored in the open roadstead at Christmas Island. Because the bottom is so steep to (deep water right up to the shore), it was necessary to anchor very close to shore on a hard, rocky bottom. There was a surge coming from the west breaking on the shore. Having to anchor so close to shore, this had the potential of setting us on a rock shore quicker than we could say, *"We've got a problem!"*

I had noticed on the chart that there were buoys set aside at Christmas Island for anchoring the phosphate ships. Phosphate mining is their only industry. These buoys had long chain leads to anchors in very deep water, plus chain-to-shore fastenings. That fact should have alerted me to the condition of the bottom.

There was one other boat anchored there. Its skipper told me he had four anchors down. This is not the sort of anchorage I can sleep in. Standing a twenty-four hour anchor watch is not my idea of rest. *"No rest at anchor, stay at sea!"* was my thought. Within thirty minutes of dropping the anchor, it was up and we were running in the beautiful trade wind to the Cocos Keeling Islands.

June 4: The wind was east southeast at fifteen knots and the swell was nine feet.

June 5: The wind increased to twenty-five knots, gusting to thirty-five knots from the south. We had a twenty-foot swell coming from south southwest to south southeast. There were thunderstorms and heavy rain. Our position was 11 degrees 15 minutes south and 102 degrees 08 minutes east. With that weather, I was glad we had left Christmas Island. Conditions there at that time would have had to be getting very interesting with the big swell and storms coming into the anchorage!

At nightfall, we were fifteen miles from Cocos Keeling. In good weather, we would have had to heave to overnight and close in the morning. I figured that with a strong south wind and stormy conditions, the anchorage would be lousy. Indeed it was, as I learned later. I talked to friends who had arrived there in daylight that very same day. That night they experienced a three- to four-foot chop in the lagoon. They had to snug up as close as possible to Direction Island in order to get out of the worst of it.

That night, we had a most unusual experience! We were sailing along, nicely reefed down. I was topside in a very heavy rain which was beating on the sea. The rain calmed the sea wave considerably, but, by no means, stopped or slowed down ***Mermaid***. In fact, ***Mermaid*** was doing quite nicely with the fifty-square-foot storm jib and the third reef in the main. Visibility was about nothing. It was as black as can be imagined with lightning flashes, giving a sailor the feeling one has on such a little boat in such a big ocean in all that wind, lightning and rain. That feeling is called ***respect.***

All around us, as far as I could see, the ocean glowed with a green-white luminescence. It seemed as if ***Mermaid*** were on a carpet of light in the blackest of space. It was downright eerie! If only for a moment, I thought that we might be going through a time warp to a new dimension. Then, it dawned on me what was going on. The ocean in this area is rich in bioluminescent plankton and other similar creatures. The hard-beating rain was exposing them to the air or stimulating them in some other way to make them glow. There was not one spot in my range of vision where the ocean did not glow that night. My world seemed so small in that cocoon of black rain and occasional lightning, with green-white light glowing in the water all around.

MAURITIUS

June 6: We continued by Cocos Keeling with a thirty-knot wind gusting to forty knots and a south swell of twenty feet. The sky was overcast and became broken later. Our position was 11 degrees 39 minutes south and 97 degrees 43 minutes east.

June 7: The wind decreased to twenty to twenty-five knots from the southeast and the sky was overcast with heavy rain. ***Mermaid*** was en route to Mauritius.

June 8: The waves were south to southeast and the swell had moderated. The sky was clear to scattered clouds and we had a good sailing ocean.

June 9 and 10: We had a clear sky with a south wind at twenty knots and a south swell.

June 11: The wind was from the south at twenty knots with a wind shift to east southeast at sunset. It was mostly overcast all day. Our position was 12 degrees 54 minutes south and 93 degrees 34 minutes east. We saw a freighter going northeast that day.

June 12: The wind was south southeast at twenty knots.

June 13: The wind shifted to south southwest at fifteen to twenty knots and we were on a close reach. Our course was 270 degrees true. There was a five-tenths cloud cover condition and it looked totally clear in the west.

June 14: The wind was twenty to thirty knots southeast to south. The waves were six to twelve feet, also southeast and south. There was seven-tenths cloud cover and occasional light showers. The cabin temperature was 74 degrees F. At night, the wind got stronger.

June 15, 16 and 17: The wind was twenty knots from the southeast. The waves were eight feet. The sky had cumulus clouds with a five-tenths cover. Our position on the 15th was 15 degrees 22 minutes south and 78 degrees 48 minutes east.

The seas were sparkling (a deep blue water with a brillant white, white cap and bright sunlight reflecting off the wave movement) on the 17th.

June 18: The wind dropped to six to eight knots with three-foot waves and a swell to seven feet. There were showers around us with gusting wind. In the evening, a squall line of showers passed across us with wind from the southeast to thirty knots. Later, the wind was down to fifteen to twenty knots, southeast, with more showers coming from the southeast. Our position was 16 degrees 51 minutes south and 73 degrees 04 minutes east.

June19, 1992: The wind was south southeast to thirty knots. Our variation was 18 degrees west. We had a five-tenths cloud cover with showers.

June 20: We had variable conditions. Wind was southeast blowing from five to thirty knots with rain showers. We sighted our first land sentinel of the Indian Ocean. A tropic bird hovered over us and screamed its call, as if to say, *"Land is ahead!"* We were six hundred forty miles from Mauritius at the time. Various tropic birds have notified us of land ahead when we were five hundred to seven hundred miles from Brazil, Hiva Oa, Australia, and now Mauritius. We'd been a bit closer to the shore when we encountered our first tropic bird off Ecuador. Almost anywhere in the tropics, such a bird seems to be there to say, *"Hello!"* Usually, it doesn't just fly by. More often, it will fly around the boat or hover and give its screeching call. How great it is to see one of them come to say, *"Hello!"* Although, it might be saying, *"What are you doing on my sea?"* It seems like a welcoming ambassador to me.

June 21: The wind was south southeast at twenty knots. There were scattered clouds.

June 22: The wind was east to southeast at fifteen knots. It was a sparkling day.

June 23: The wind was southeast from twenty to twenty-five knots. The clouds were a broken condition with showers.

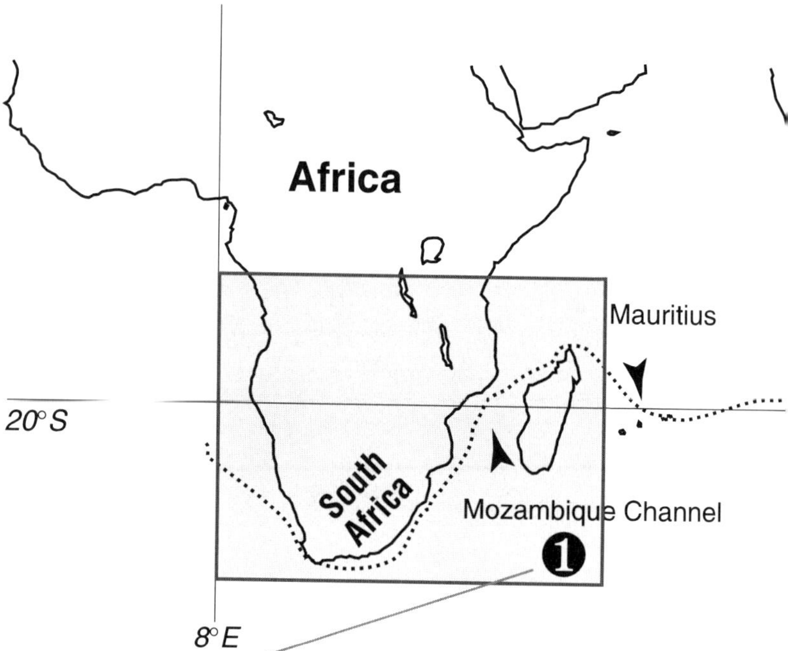
Africa
Mauritius
20° S
South Africa
Mozambique Channel
1
8° E

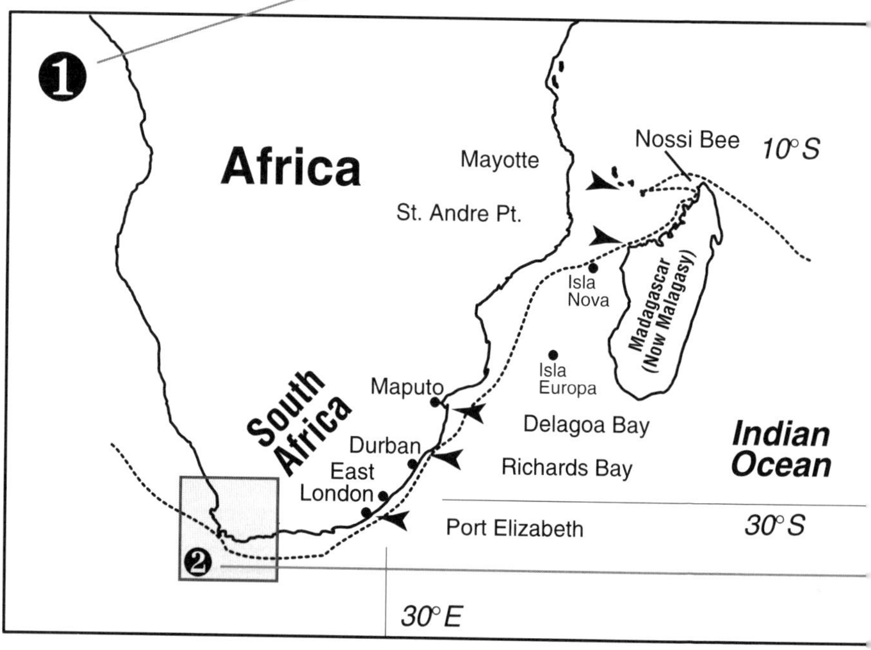
1
Africa
Mayotte
St. Andre Pt.
Nossi Bee
10° S
Isla Nova
Madagascar (Now Malagasy)
Isla Europa
Maputo
South Africa
Delagoa Bay
Durban
East London
Richards Bay
Indian Ocean
Port Elizabeth
30° S
2
30° E

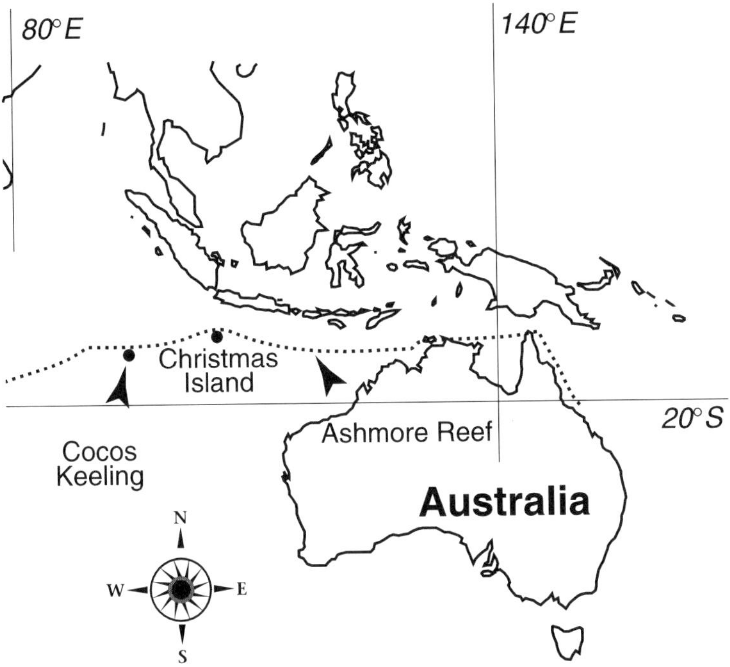
80° E
140° E
Christmas
Island
20° S
Cocos
Keeling
Ashmore Reef
Australia
N
W
E
S

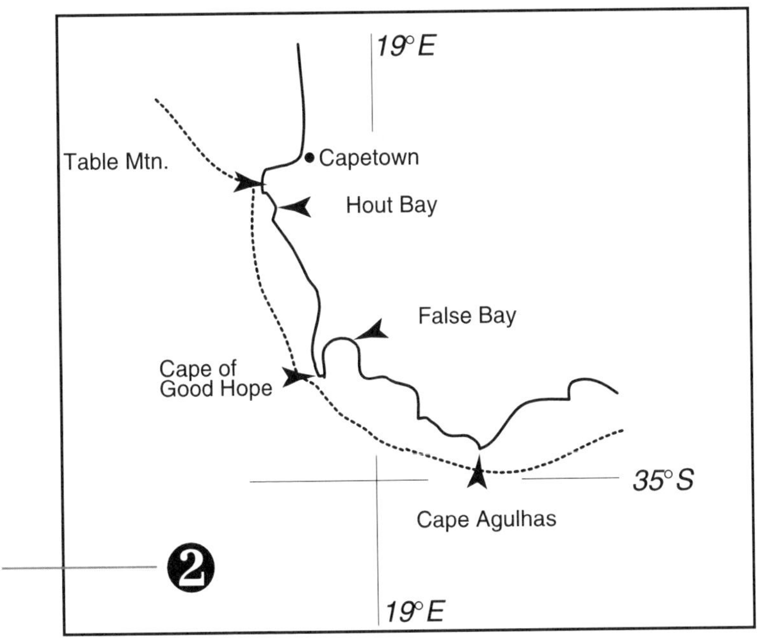
19° E
Table Mtn.
Capetown
Hout Bay
False Bay
Cape of
Good Hope
35° S
Cape Agulhas
2
19° E

Our position was 19 degrees 06 minutes south and 64 degrees 59 minutes east.

June 24: The weather cleared in the morning. The wind was east southeast at fifteen to twenty knots.

June 25: We had a nice day. The wind was east northeast to east southeast at twenty to twenty-five knots. We sighted Mauritius at sunset, about twenty miles away, concluding one of the finest sails of all the oceans we had crossed. We had had strong trade wind conditions all the way, once we were off the Australian shelf. ***What a fantastic ocean!*** Our experiences there washed away all the bad sailing we had endured with the El Nino effect in the Pacific. We had a great sail on a great ocean in a great trade wind!

We closed on a bearing to Round Island, the furthest small island north of the main islands, and the north end of the shelf. By 2200 LT , I had run my DR to the north end of Round Island. Having done so, I expected to see the twenty-nine mile light indicated on my chart to verify that we had passed Round Island. But there was no light! I didn't dare head south toward the city of Port Louis without knowing for sure that we were west of Round Island. Even though we could see the loom from city lights and get a bearing, I wasn't willing to risk the obstructions on the shelf until I had better confirmation of our position relative to the island than a loom of lights. Going very far west past Round Island would have meant beating back to Mauritius against the strong trades. So, we heaved to for a while.

June 26: While we were heaved to, ***Mermaid*** was in such a position that the island was directly in line with the Port Louis loom of lights. At 0200 LT, the waning third-quarter moon came up. Between the moon and the loom of lights, I could see Round Island with my binoculars. The island appeared as a round hill which blocked out part of the horizon loom. When the moon came up, it silhouetted the side of the island towards us enough for me to identify it. I could also see the curvature of the hill in the loom. With this bearing, I was able to determine our position relative to the island.

At 0300 LT, we rounded Round Island and turned south. By dawn, we were passing the last small island before the main island. That was where the twenty-nine mile light was supposed to be. The old light tower was there, but with no light. My chart was a few years old. But the land is there. That is all that mattered.

That afternoon, we sailed into Port Louis and tied to the seawall at the end of the customs jetty. Our clearance in began almost immediately with four or five people aboard. It went smoothly up to the time we talked to the immigration man.

"You don't have a visa," he said.

I replied, *"That's true. Sailing at the speed we were going, we didn't have time to apply for a visa and receive it in the mail before we were sailing again. I hope that you will issue a visa here. If you can't, we will sail on. You can see that we are here as tourists and would like to stay."*

He told us to come to his office the next day. They would decide then if they would issue a visa.

In many countries of the world, including Mauritius, people wear long pants or dresses and appear very conservative in their dress. They don't let it all hang out so to speak. Usually, they are offended when visitors wear revealing clothing. Some sailors dress like ragamuffins in order to illustrate their independence and relaxed attitude in general. This can offend the natives in these conservative places. This is not necessarily true of all places, but it is in some places. ***Dress like the natives and you can't go wrong!***

The next day, we dressed like the natives. I wore a shirt and pants, and Marione wore a dress. We went to immigration where we got a visa for a two-week stay. Later, we extended it for another thirty days. That was as long as we wanted to stay. I'm sure we could have stayed longer had we wanted to.

FRIGHT

It was a real scare
We found out the thieves were there
They easily came into secured air
And boldly came aboard knowing we were there
And I don't think they planned us to be spared.

Luckily for us the hatch was quick to shut
and being so strong one could trust
And my wife was so alert and made a fuss
That I got up and checked it out in a rush
For they were ready to come and make a bust.

They jumped on the cabin trunk and ran to the hatch
Trying to push it open as I was pushing it back
The adrenaline ran through my arms and hands
And I closed that hatch like a muscle man
And there they did stand knowing
they had missed their plan.

A yacht can stay tied to the customs seawall in Mauritius as long as a person likes, or until the area becomes crowded with a lot of boats clearing in. When we arrived, there was one other sailboat from South Africa at the seawall, so we decided to stay there. The area is secured with an eight-foot, chain-link fence with barbed wire on top. There is a security gate with police on guard twenty-four hours a day. A police station is inside the fence, fifty yards from where we were tied, but it was blocked from our view by a spoil bank of mud that had been removed from the harbor some time previously.

The secured area is a farce! The fence is on the land side of the seawall. This leaves a convenient walkway down the seawall to the moorings and docks, an easy access with no guard! In this setting, we came as close as we ever had to being hurt or even murdered.

From Darwin to Mauritius, we had spent thirty-eight days at sea. This was our first night in port. Because we thought we were in a secured area, the hatch was open forward. The hatch aft was also open, as was the porthole. ***Mermaid*** does not have a companionway. When I built ***Mermaid***, I felt a companionway would be a weakness in a small boat in heavy weather. Instead there is a step over the trunk. Then, one goes down the hatch opening to go below, using a six-step stair. That night, I was sleeping in the bow while Marione was writing letters.

Around 2200 LT, Marione came in and said, *"I think someone is watching the boat!"*

I said, *"No way. We're in a secured area,"* and rolled back over.

Five minutes later, she was back saying that she was sure someone was watching the boat. So, I got up to check. Sure enough, a fellow had come down the seawall from town and was fishing with a line. He would fish forward of ***Mermaid*** and then fish aft of ***Mermaid***, looking in the porthole and paying much too much attention to ***Mermaid***. I went up the hatch and took a good look at him. He continued to fish. Coming down, I decided that it wouldn't hurt to lock up. So, I reached up to push the hatch shut. The fellow knew that the game was up! ***He ran onto the boat and grabbed the hatch,*** trying to push it open. The adrenaline was running at that point and I managed to shut the hatch. Marione grabbed our lock bar and secured the hatch, then ran forward to drop the forward hatch. I closed the porthole.

There were two of them and they had a pistol. We were locked in and they were locked out. The fellow who had tried to push the hatch open was so mad that he hammered on the hatch with his fist. All I could think of was that it was the end of the month and he must have had a car payment due on the first of the month.

The other fellow was trying to pry up the forward hatch. No way possible! It is made from two-inch mahogany dogged with one-half-inch stainless steel bolts and wing nuts, and secured by one-half-inch thick stainless steel angle lagged into two inches of white oak. The window in the hatch is one-inch Plexiglas. The aft hatch is constructed in the same way. The porthole glass is three quarters of an inch thick. It is a freighter porthole. The only way to get in when it is secured is with an axe. The guy at the aft hatch was fearless. As he looked down the hatch, I showed him the three-foot machete waiting for him at the bottom of the ladder. He jerked even harder on the hatch to get in.

Having a gun makes a man very brave. What is it that they say? *"God created man, but Sam Colt made them equal."* We carry a forty-five pound longbow with steel-pointed arrows, which we strung. Customs will confiscate a gun almost everywhere, as they had our gun here. But, they have no problem with a bow and arrows. Mace is also good to have aboard.

Both of our visitors looked in through the porthole. I shone my flashlight in their faces. Sadly, they apparently didn't mind if we could identify them. They told me they were the police. I told them to come back tomorrow. They spent about fifteen minutes on the boat, trying to get in. They apparently wanted nothing topside. ***Mermaid's*** dinghy motor and generator were there, locked. They are the reason for the longbow. The generator and motor are locked in full view of the porthole. I can shoot anyone trying to steal them with the bow from inside. The raid was unsuccessful so our visitors finally left. Had they gotten in, we would have been in deep trouble! All of this happened in a supposedly secured area, just fifty yards from the police station.

I feel that securing yourself in your boat is one of the best ways to prevent trouble like this in a foreign port. The thief can't get in to you and your possessions. If he does, you have the first advantage of attack. In a foreign country, avoiding attack is the best course of action. A native who is a criminal may have more rights than you do. I reported the incident to the police the next day. They were unconcerned. There was no increase in security on the seawall walkway.

We stayed at the seawall two more days, securing the ***Mermaid*** at night. We had no other incidents. The third day, we moved to Grand Bay. We anchored in a lovely bay with a yacht club and good stores for provisioning. Prices were reasonable. We could get everything we needed.

The basic monetary unit in Mauritius is the rupee. The exchange was 15 rupees to $1.00 U.S. Some of the prices were: one kilo of potatoes for 5 rupees, one kilo of onions for 9 rupees, three oranges for 10 rupees, bananas for 1 rupee each, and apples for 4 rupees each. Cabbage, squash, papaya, and pineapple were 10 rupees each.

Good bus transportation to Port Louis gave us a pretty ride through the sugarcane fields. There are tremendous rock piles near the fields, testifying to the hard work in clearing lava fields to plant sugar. Mauritius reminded us of Fiji. Indian serfs had also been brought here by the British to work the sugar. As a result, there is a large Asian Indian population. This means the women wear colorful, long, flowing dresses with exotic jewelry having a lot of gold in it. It also means Moslem mosques and Hindu temples, as well as Christian churches.

Here, the tourist experiences many cultures in one location. Cultures from India, Europe, Africa, and the Orient coexist. While watching TV, we saw one program in English, the next in French, and then one in an Indian dialect. Most people speak three or four languages here, and it doesn't matter which language the show is in. People are friendly. We enjoyed the island.

We rented a mo-ped on two occasions. Marione jumped on the seat behind me and we rode a great part of the island this way. We saw beautiful beaches, blue water, palm trees, jagged mountains, and nice houses. The variation in elevation is such that one can go to the hills to cool off. One may even need a sweater there to keep warm. Then, one can drop back to sea level to warm up again.

One day, we were hiking the roads and the paths of Grand Bay. While walking through a wooded area with fields, we happened on a bunch of credit cards lying on the ground. We thought someone might be missing them so we decided to pick them up. It appeared that a wallet had been stolen and the contents dumped. We picked up everything we could find, including a visa, a mastercard, and a couple of other cards from a Scotland bank. Among them was a paper with an address on it. It looked to be a London address, but, then again, it could have been a London Street here in Mauritius, if there was such a street.

Before we took them to a police station to be lost in the bureaucracy, we thought we would pursue the address, as there was also a telephone number. We spoke to the guard at the gate of one of the hotels. He thought there was a London Street a few blocks down the road.

So we walked down the road, looking for the street. After passing a number of streets without finding what we were looking for, we approached another fellow on the street. He assured us that there was no street by that name. We walked back to the hotel and decided to go into the hotel to the desk to find out if the telephone number was a Mauritius number. We chose the same hotel where we had originally talked to the guard at the gate. Arriving at the desk, we discovered that the number must indeed be a London number, so, we gave up on the idea of looking for a local address to find the owner.

On a sudden hunch, I asked, *"Do you have a George Smith registered here?"* giving the name on the credit card.

The desk clerk looked at the register and said, *"Why, yes, we do."*

I couldn't believe that, of all the hotels in Mauritius, we had walked into the very hotel where George Smith was staying. What luck! Was this the right man? I asked the clerk to ring George's room and I talked to him on the house phone. He was sleeping when we rang, although the hour was about eleven in the morning.

"Hi George! Have you, by chance, lost your credit cards?" I asked.

"I don't believe so," he replied.

"Do you do business with Scotland Bank?" I continued to question.

"Yes, I do," he answered.

"Then you have lost your credit cards. I'm here in the lobby to give them back to you."

"This is a joke!" he exclaimed.

"No, it's not a joke. Come to the lobby," I said.

When he got to the lobby, we could see the kind of night he had had by the size of his hangover. While putting on his pants to come downstairs, he had discovered that his wallet was really missing. He told us that he had picked up a gal who had spent the night. Before leaving in the morning, she must have taken his wallet. He got his credit cards back before he knew they were missing. How's that for efficiency? Needless to say, George was thankful to get his cards back and he thanked us. We went away happy and feeling good about being able to do this good deed.

While we were in Grand Bay, Frank Hedges, a Canadian single-hander came in from Singapore on his yacht ***Niatross.*** He had been in the South China Sea, a known area for piracy. It was interesting to note from our conversations that the freighters in that area run with floodlights shining across their decks. They do this to spot pirates coming over the side. They will also often run without running lights to make it more difficult for pirates to determine the course they are on. We were to meet Frank again in Richards Bay, South Africa. There was also a German trimaran on its way to Africa. Most of the other yachts were French boats from Reunion, a French island one hundred miles southwest of Mauritius.

One South African boat had sailed to Mauritius from Port Elizabeth, South Africa. He had had a real beat over thirty days to Reunion, and then on to Mauritius. His boat had been beaten so hard by the weather that a wave had ***cracked one of his half-inch thick,*** eight by twelve inch Plexiglas portholes. There was a lesson in that about the power of the sea!

We had stayed in Mauritius for forty days when we decided to continue our travels. We thought about going to Malagasy (Madagascar), but we were concerned about all the people with no food on South Malagasy that we had been hearing about from news broadcasts. We assumed that that situation prevailed all over the island so we were uncertain about going to that country. However, our South African friend told us that a lot of cruisers from his area go to Nossi Bee, an island of Malagasy on the west northwest side, and almost adjoining the mainland of Malagasy with the town of Hellsville. He said that the diving there was great. It is untouched and not at all expensive.

Another option we had was to go to Mayotte, a French island in the Comoros group, which was about nine hundred miles away. We hadn't heard much about it, other than it is expensive. We decided to sail to Mayotte anyway and see what it is like. Then if things sounded good, we'd go on to Nossi Bee. If not, we would continue on to South Africa.

Since there were French and Malagasy Consulates on Mauritius, we thought we would look into getting a visa prior to our arrival on Mayotte. So, we went to the French Consulate. There, we were informed that it would take thirty days to get the visa. So, we threw away the application and hoped we could still visit Mayotte when we got there. Since we weren't sure whether we would go to Malagasy or not, we passed on that visa. By chance, that proved to be smart. We learned later that it didn't matter if a person had a visa when arriving at Hellsville, Nossi Bee Island, Malagasy. Immigration sells each person a visa when he arrives, even if one was purchased before arrival.

It was not required to obtain a South African visa. We just had to send a letter to immigration, telling them when we expected to arrive. We sent that letter from Mauritius.

MAYOTTE

August 8, 1992: We moved Mermaid back to Port Louis in order to clear out of Mauritius.

August 10: We departed Port Louis at 1130 LT en route to Mayotte. The wind was southeast at fifteen knots. The waves were three feet high with an ocean swell of six feet both from the east and southeast.

August 11: Our course was 324 degrees true. The wind was southeast at twenty knots. The waves were three to six feet and the sky was overcast.

August 12: The sky cleared and the wind was east at ten knots. We sailed in an unorganized, close, vertical, wave pattern. We sighted a freighter going south southwest.

August 13: We had a southwest wind at twenty-five knots with rain. There was an overcast to broken condition in the afternoon, and the wind dropped to twenty knots. The waves were south at six feet and the ocean swell was nine feet. Our position was 16 degrees 31 minutes south and 54 degrees 30 minutes east. There were twenty dolphins running with us today.

August 14: The wind was from the south blowing up to twenty knots and the waves were south to southeast at three to six feet. The cloud cover was broken and it was nice sailing.

August 15: The sky cleared in the morning and then returned to an eight-tenths cover in the afternoon. The wind was fifteen knots and the waves were three to six feet, both southeast to south.

August 16, 1992: We had a clear sky with haze. We were thirty-five miles from Malagasy, closing the northern end of the island. The wind was southeast at twenty-five knots and the waves were six to nine feet. We saw a bird that was new to us, perhaps a young albatross. It was white with gray across thc top of its wings. There was also black on the leading and trailing edges on its wings. It was bigger than the average bird. A twenty-foot whale also jumped out of the water as we passed. Our position was 12 degrees 58 minutes south and 48 degrees 06 minutes east.

August 17: We were having a good passage with the sails reefed down. The wind was southeast at twenty to thirty knots, gusting to thirty-five knots occasionally. The sky was clear and the waves were southeast to south with a short-spaced six to twelve footer. We rounded the north coast of Malagasy in haze with the wind patterns influenced by the land mass.

August 18: We sailed off the west side of the island of Malagasy. The wind was east to southeast at ten knots and less, dropping with a calm sea. In this location, downwind from the land, with our noses accustomed to the fresh air of the sea, the aroma of land filled our nostrils with the fragrances of burning wood, farm animals, and other activities of man, as we passed on our way to Mayotte. ***Whew!***

August 19: It was a beautiful, clear day. There was a very light wind from the southwest to south southwest and we motor-sailed.

August 20: The wind was south southwest to southwest at twenty knots. We arrived at the Mayotte northeast channel at 1300 LT. Mayotte is enclosed with an almost solid reef on the east and north sides. With the southwest wind, I chose to close on the northeast channel which appeared to be the least nerve-wracking approach to get through the reef. As I attempted to align ***Mermaid*** with the mountain range to get the compass course bearing to go through the reef, I found that I couldn't pick out the peak of the front range very easily. The range is made up of two mountain peaks in line, one behind the other. The front range, less lofty than the one further away, blended into the further range so that it was not easily identified. So I tracked in on the visible back range with the correct compass bearing, verifying our position with a pair of intersecting bearings from known landmarks. This assured me that the two posts which finally became visible sticking up in front of us were indeed on the ends of the reef and designated the opening.

Sometime later, I had a discussion with another yachtsman who had faced the very same problem of not being able to discern the front range as he entered this port. ***He was equipped with satellite navigation electronics.*** I was interested to learn just how he had handled this problem. It never occurred to him to take visual bearings using known points of reference in order to plot a position. Instead, he waited about an hour to obtain a satellite navigation position even though he could see the land. This illustrates that over-dependence on electronics can lull a navigator into forgetting about other available navigation tools. Allowing this to happen is not wise.

Once through the reef, we found a good channel south to a good anchorage in the port of Dzaoudzi, about fifteen miles south down the reef. We anchored behind a small island with a volcanic crater, about a mile from the main island. The main island is mountainous. However, these mountains are not jagged, but rounded and worn. We didn't see much cultivation. There are towns on both sides of the harbor, one on the island with the crater and the other on the main island. Clearance in was the easiest and fastest of all the places we visited. The port captain also handled both customs and immigration. He could have cared less whether we had visas in hand. One stop did it all!

We could stay as long as we wanted to-or, I should say, as long as we could afford it! Mayotte, being a French island, is very expensive. The exchange rate was 4.5 francs to $1.00 U.S. One cabbage was 10 francs, if one could be found. Three medium potatoes were 14 francs, a very small bag of popcorn was 8 francs, and diesel fuel was 3.8 francs per liter. Most boats at Mayotte were from Reunion and South Africa. They did their provisioning in Malagasy, then came here to enjoy the anchorage and hiking trails. There were also occasional military ships coming into the harbor because the French Foreign Legion has its Indian Ocean base here.

We went ashore and hiked around the ridge of the crater. A lake had formed at the bottom of the crater and the higher ground in the crater was cultivated with coconuts. After hiking the crater ridge, we continued on the deserted, mountain ridges to the end of the island where there is an airport. Along the way, we dropped down into sandy coves which were mostly deserted as well.

When we passed the airport, we stopped by the weather station to get an accurate setting for our barometer. On our return to ***Mermaid***, I reset our barometer. This assisted us greatly in our passage to and around South Africa.

Observing and talking to the natives of these islands is a cultural experience. They are very interesting. The native women dress in bright colors and long robes. They use a yellowish-white powder on their faces to enhance their beauty. Someone not used to this appearance might think they'd fallen, face first, into some yellowish mud! I wanted to take a picture of one of the natives, but did not because she was shy of the camera.

The island also offers the best anchorage of the whole Comoros group. As a bonus, we got a lot of good information for going down the Mozambique Channel and visiting Malagasy. We found out from some cruisers who had just come from Malagasy that there were not any food shortages on the north end of the island, even though on the south end people were short of food. With this information, we decided to visit the north end of Malagasy.

MALAGASY (MADAGASCAR)

August 31, 1992: We cleared Mayotte and went out the northeast channel, heading for Hellsville on the island of Nossi Bee, Malagasy. Our course was 105 degrees true. The wind was southeast at five knots and the waves were small with a swell of three feet or less. We were motor-sailing.

September 1: Our course was 112 degrees true. The wind was south southeast at five knots. The wave action was very unorganized because of a three-foot swell converging from the south, southeast, and the northeast. These swells were coming from different directions and they were not caused by any particular wind pattern. The barometer was 1017 millibars. We enjoyed a beautiful, deep red sunset with a clear sky.

September 2: We sighted and closed Nossi Bee, anchoring at Hellsville at 1430 LT. There were seven boats in the anchorage: French, South African, New Zealand, British, Italian and U.S. Some had come south through the Red Sea from the Mediterranean.

Clearance was easy, starting with the port captain. He did all the paperwork, bringing immigration and customs to his office while we went to the bank to pick up Malagasy francs. I purchased Malagasy francs using American Express travelers checks. The bank teller took the checks and gave me Malagasy francs, thinking that the transaction was finished. However, I had not signed the checks. I tried to explain in my limited French something that I thought was very obvious. Apparently, she didn't understand since she brought her supervisor over. He also did not see a problem, but knew a person who worked at the bank who could speak a little English. Talking to him, the light dawned and they realized it was necessary to have the checks signed before they were good. I love these remote areas to cruise. It reminds me of how uncomplicated life can be. The Malagasy exchange rate was 1782 francs to $1.00 U.S. The cost of clearance was 71000 francs. That included visas, which are sold there, even if a person had one in hand before entry.

We rented a car and drove around the island of Nossi Bee. Our tour of the island was an enlightening experience. It is beautiful and undeveloped. The people are friendly and break into smiles easily. We noticed that sanitation is a problem with a need for public toilets. This problem also exists all over the world.

Even though people were starving in the south because of a very dry year, there were plenty of fruits and vegetables in the markets in the north. All could be had for good prices. Dealing in the market worked best when we paid for each item as we picked it up, and didn't make the dealer do any math to total purchases. That seemed to cause confusion.

As we looked around, it felt like a cultural step back in history. We saw the ancient Arab dhows being built and used for cargo. With its lateen (triangular) sail, this type of boat was one of the first sailing vessels built that had good windward performance. We also saw fishermen using outrigger canoes with sails.

We were eating in a restaurant one day when some young ladies came in and asked us to take their pictures. We happily obliged. They had designs on their faces, using the same yellow-white powder we had seen in Mayotte. Then, they told us they hoped we would pay them a little something for their pictures.

"Do you want the money, or would you prefer to have a picture when the film is developed?" I asked.

All four of them said together that they'd like a picture. They gave us an address. When we were in South Africa, we had the pictures developed and mailed them to these great kids. I hope they received them.

RICHARDS BAY, SOUTH AFRICA

September 13, 1992: We cleared Nossi Bee and cruised in a leisurely fashion down the coast to St. Andre Point in the Mozambique Channel. The wind was variable. It was predominately a land breeze in the night and then a sea breeze during the day. We got to sail part of the time, but mostly motor-sailed.

On the northwest coast, there are reefs on a shallow shelf, which extend up to twenty miles offshore. The French survey charts leave unanswered questions, such as, the navigablc dcpths over some of these reefs. On the charts, there are depths marked, that appear safe for navigation. There are also markings of shipwrecks in some of the very same spots. These were apparently added after the survey charts were published. This hardly instills confidence in the charts! Nevertheless, we found that with a small craft and good seamanship, there was no problem in cruising this area.

As we continued south along the coast, we saw many lovely, remote, uncruised areas with many anchorages. We didn't see many boats in this great, virgin, cruising ground. It may be the South African and the Reunion Island cruisers best kept secret.

September 16: We continued moving towards Saint Andre Point while we considered our options for our sail to South Africa.

While we were in Mayotte, we had had a good conversation with Lucy, a delivery skipper who had been around the Cape of Good Hope twenty-six times. She had also frequently sailed the Mozambique Channel up to Kalefi in Kenya. She told us that she hardly ever got blasted at sea by a storm from the southwest (sou'wester) anymore because of her method of navigation when going south in the Mozambique Channel to Richards Bay, South Africa.

Since the weather seems to be worst from Saint Andre Point south, Lucy takes her first run to Juan de Nova Island just southwest of Saint Andre Point, where there is a good protected anchorage, sheltered from a southwest wind. If all is well, she continues down to Isle Europa, where she can hang an anchor on a reef with protection from the south and southwest wind afforded by the reef. This puts her in a good sailing position to take advantage of a southeast wind to make her final leg to Richards Bay.

Her rule of thumb for leaving Europa is based on the fact that it usually takes three days for a sou'wester to get from Cape Town to Richards Bay. So, she figures the number of days before the storm gets to Cape Town then adds three more days. This total is the number of days to get to protection before the next storm. Should a storm approach faster than anticipated, she has the option of going to Delagoa Bay to anchor off the point, just south of the harbor approach to Maputo, Mozambique. She then can proceed to Richards Bay when the sou'wester passes.

She uses a barometer to predict the weather she can expect. Her system is simple. A barometer drop of five millibars is no big deal. A drop of ten millibars relates to fifteen- to twenty-five knot-wind, a drop of fifteen millibars relates to thirty- to forty-knot wind, and a drop of twenty millibars relates to a forty-knot wind plus.

Another option for sailing in this part of the world going south, is to move west across the channel to the old clipper ship route indicated on the pilot charts. Coming north up the channel, this route kept to the east side in order to catch the counter-current that flows east of Isle Europa and Juan de Nova, then west of Saint Andre Point. Headed south, the sailors would look for the Mozambique Current on the west side of the channel, just off the east coast of Africa. This allowed the current to help push them through the channel.

Since we were sailing in September, the weather had moderated. We no longer expected to encounter severe southern hemisphere winter storms that far north. So, we opted for the clipper ship route with the option to anchor off Delagoa Bay by Maputo if needed.

Once underway, it didn't take long to see why the clipper ships had used the east side of the Mozambique Channel to go north. That countercurrent must be two knots sometimes, judging by our north set. From Saint Andre Point, we set our heading toward Juan de Nova with plans to stop there, however, the north-flowing countercurrent set us north faster than expected. When it became obvious that we'd have a night arrival there, we opted to continue to the middle of the channel before turning ***Mermaid*** to the south. By so doing, we hoped to get into the south-flowing Mozambique Current and take advantage of it.

September 17 and 18, 1992: The wind was light and variable. We motor-sailed at 1200 rpm in order to conserve fuel. Back in Nossi Bee, I hadn't topped up the diesel fuel because I had expected the Mozambique Channel to be windy.

September 19: As we continued to motor-sail, our position was 17 degrees 01 minute south and 41 degrees 16 minutes east. There was a long, south swell of nine to twelve feet.

September 20: With smooth water, we continued our slow motor-sail. In the evening, the wind increased to ten knots from the north. ***Mermaid*** began moving under sail power again. The waves were from three to six feet, a bit high for the wind. We had a clear sky. The barometer read 1015 millibars.

September 21: The Indian Ocean high was centered over Malagasy. The barometer read 1020 millibars. The wind was northeast at fifteen to twenty knots with waves from three to six feet. We had good sailing while running the clipper ship route from Zanzibar as we experienced a one-knot current as well. The sky was clear. Our position was 19 degrees 03 minutes south and 38 degrees 37 minutes east. Our course was 208 degrees true.

September 22: The wind was northeast at twenty to twenty-five knots with waves to six feet and a swell to twelve feet, both northeast. A low passed south of us, crossing the Mozambique Channel at Maputo with a thirty-five-knot wind. The barometer dipped to 1006 millibars in the low. We enjoyed a clear sky and a beautiful, red sunset.

September 23: The wind dropped to calm. The waves became unorganized, coming from all different directions. There was a swell from the east at fifteen feet. Our position was 22 degrees 15 minutes south and 38 degrees east.

September 24: We motor-sailed once more over a lumpy sea with vertical wave action from different directions. The wind was five knots or less.

September 25: The wind was five knots shifting from the east to northeast to southeast. The sea was almost flat. We had a clear sky with the barometer standing at 1017 millibars. We motored at 1200 rpm. Our position was 25 degrees 24 minutes south and 35 degrees 55 minutes east.

September 26: In the morning, the wind came from the southeast at fifteen to twenty knots. We sailed along after three days of motoring. We saw four whales lazing along on the surface. The waves and swell were six feet. Our position was 28 degrees 47 minutes south and 32 degrees 08 minutes east.

September 27: The wind was eight knots from the southeast. The waves were three feet and a long, widely-spaced swell was twelve to fifteen feet from the southeast. The six-tenths broken cloud cover in the morning became overcast in the afternoon. The barometer stood at 1020 millibars.

The sea can change its wave pattern very quickly in the Mozambique Channel. I had not planned on so much light air this trip. Leaving Nossi Bee light on fuel cost us time. To conserve fuel, we ran at 1200 rpm. This allowed us to progress at about three knots when the wind was down. I did learn that when operating at 1200 rpm, ***Mermaid's*** Perkins model 4-108 industrial engine rated at 50 horsepower used three tenths of a gallon of fuel per hour. That relates to a horsepower output of about 6 horsepower, figuring 180 grams of diesel is used per horsepower.

September 28, 1992: ***We arrived at the customs pier*** in Richards Bay at 0630 LT. Richards Bay is the name of the harbor, not of any town in the vicinity. Clearance into South Africa is quick. The officials are efficient. Yachtsmen can stay at the customs pier for a few days, so long as there isn't an overload of boats clearing in. Once things were sorted out, we moved over to the Richards Bay Yacht Club. At high spring tide, the channel into the yacht club handled a seven-foot draft at that time. When we were there, the first two weeks were free on the floating dock. However, we preferred a buoy with more elbow room. So, we took a buoy for $22.00 U.S. per month. These buoys are located between the mainland and a sand island with some interesting wildlife. While sitting in our cockpit, we could watch monkeys walk down the island beach. What's more, a pair of sea eagles, that look very much like our bald eagle, lived there, too.

One day, while walking on the island, we watched a huge crane hunt a striking snake and then eat it. The snake had made the strategic error of getting caught on the beach. It was fascinating to watch the crane's cool procedure in dealing with the snake. I presume the snake, between two and three feet long, was poisonous. It struck professionally at the bird. However, the great crane kept its legs just out of the snake's striking range. Every so often, the crane would strike the snake's head with a crushing blow from its ten-inch, pointed beak, then, back came the crane's head as the snake would strike. But the bird continued to keep its legs and body just out of striking range.

It was easy to see that the crane had things under control. Progressively, after a number of strikes to the snake's head, the fight gradually left it. After a final strike, the crane picked up the snake and put it underwater for a few minutes, holding it there by its head. Once the snake had drowned, the crane laid it on the beach and tenderized it with crushing squeezes with its beak. Then, holding onto the end of the snake, the crane flipped its own head and neck straight up. At that point, the snake flipped straight up into the air and then it went directly down into the crane's gullet, nonstop. What a digestive tract!

The only annoyance for the yachtsmen in Richards Bay is a depot for exporting coal. With a southwest wind, soot settles on the boats. At the time of year we were there, that wind was less frequent and the advantages far outweighed that disadvantage.

There are two towns, Marrenseea and Upingany, which are very close to the yacht club. Marrenseea is about two miles away with a post office and stores. To reach it, there is a scenic walk from the yacht club with a shortcut through the woods. When we walked on this path, we saw monkeys in the trees.

Upingany is about five miles away. It also has many stores and a library. We attempted to walk there a few times, but got a lift on the road both ways each time. It was easy to catch a ride with someone at the yacht club, also. The entire area has the feeling of small-town friendliness not found in the larger cities. It is tropical there. That makes it a good place to stay warm until it warms up to the south.

These towns are very close to some magnificent game preserves. In fact, the local reservoir is inhabited by ***hippopotamuses!*** The harbor of Richards Bay is an excellent stop for the cruiser to have access to the game preserves. It's really more convenient to see these parks from here than going to them from Durban, further south along the coast. However, because of the considerable civil unrest in South Africa at the time, we elected to stay near the coast rather than go inland to visit the parks.

There are many boats at Richards Bay waiting to head around Cape Agulhas, the southernmost point of Africa, and the well-known Cape of Good Hope. A couple of them were as small as twenty-three feet. While at Richards Bay, we were all thinking ahead about the notorious waters we'd soon be navigating. Horror stories abound regarding turbulent water and giant waves which have sunk ships. These stories are true. When sailing outside the one hundred-fathom curve south from Point Dunford, just north of Richards Bay, it is possible to encounter giant waves. The Agulhas Current runs southwest in that area with two to five knots of current. The giant waves happen when a strong sou'wester comes in. They are produced by the interaction of the strong winds blowing against the strong current running in the opposite direction. That interaction causes a vertical sea. Occasionally, it has happened that two or three of these steep waves have overlapped. This produces a huge wave with a deep trough. When a vessel goes down into the trough, it is so deep that the wave towers over the bow of the vessel. When the wave crashes onto the ship with its full weight and power, it has been known to sink even the large ocean freighters!

Consequently, standard safe operating procedure for freighters in heavy weather is to move inside the one hundred-fathom curve. Standard safe operating procedure for small craft is to stay inside the one hundred-fathom curve at all times! There is less available current push, but there is the safety margin that no giant waves form inside the one hundred-fathom curve. Any vertical waves there will be much smaller.

It is obvious that there are basic strategies to consider before attempting to sail these waters. First, the time of year is important. The sailor is less likely to encounter the severe sou'westers in the summer, which, in the southern hemisphere runs from December into March. It is wise to plan a trip for that time of year in this area. It's the same principle used as when a person is picking a season for ocean travel anywhere.

Next, the weather forecasting in South Africa, particularly trying to predict the unpredictable conditions there, is a real job! The fronts are always predicted. Nevertheless, occasional twelve-hour squalls occur that are missed in the forecast. The best approach, in order to go through this region with an easy mind and avoiding bad weather, is to jump from port to port down the southeast coast of South Africa between fronts. That means a person could have stops from Richards Bay to Durban, then from Durban to East London, then on to Port Elizabeth.

After arriving at Port Elizabeth, the most dangerous area has been transited. Even at that, it is most dangerous only outside the one hundred-fathom curve. From Port Elizabeth west to Cape Town, there is no longer a current problem. There are also anchorages available at closer intervals for protection from strong sou'westers. Most of these anchorages give protection only from the initial blast of the front. As the wind shifts and moderates in the course of the storm, these anchorages become the windward shore. As this wind shift is observed, it is necessary to move out of the anchorage and sail west with this favoring wind.

Going west, before reaching Cape Agulhas, there is a shallow shelf coming off the cape. It is plenty deep above this shelf, but not as deep as it is off the shelf. Looking at the chart, one might think this is a choppy wave area. It is not! For some reason, this shelf has a calmer sea than further offshore in deeper water. It is safe to sail right across it.

DURBAN, SOUTH AFRICA

November 13, 1992: On Friday the thirteenth, we left Richards Bay on a high tide. A sou'wester was forecast on Sunday, but we expected to reach Durban before it arrived. The barometer read 1013 millibars. Four hours later, a squall came in from the southwest at twenty-five knots. We beat to windward in a short, vertical sea which made any progress very difficult. Where we were, the waves were from six to nine feet. Beyond the one hundred-fathom curve, they were much larger. Toward the shore, the waves were much smaller.

November 14: The wind dropped to ten knots and the waves also dropped. Both were from the southwest. ***Mermaid*** motored on a direct course to Durban. As the day progressed, the wind continued to get lighter. It eventually dropped to five knots and the sea flattened.

We arrived in Durban just before midnight and tied to the customs dock. We were required to clear in and out of every port in South Africa. We also had to have permission from the port authority to enter and leave the harbor. This is done with the VHF radio on arrival at the port. We cleared in and moved to an anchorage off the yacht club.

While we were there, the exchange rate was 3 rand to $1.00 U.S. The Point Yacht Club charged 20 rand per week for each person who used its showers and facilities. Additionally, it charged 20 rand per week to dock the dinghy and use water.

Durban is a clean city and a pleasant place to visit. There is an interesting museum and a good library for reading. This makes it a good place to catch up on what's happening in the world. There are also many movie theaters. Movie tickets were 7 rand at the time.

Across the street from the yacht club is ***Toni's Marine Store.*** We found it a good place to do business. He carries a complete inventory of used British Admiralty charts that he obtains from the freighters that pass through the area. In turn, he offers them at a price of 5 to 11 rand each. Thus, at Toni's, a person can get British Admiralty charts for just about anywhere in the world for 11 rand or less.

When we arrived in Richards Bay, I didn't yet have any detail charts for South African waters south of Durban. So, on a road trip to Durban, I bought several charts for 5 rand each at Toni's. All of them were published by the British Admiralty and all of them were in good shape.

South Africa publishes a light list to identify its beacons, an automatic direction finder (ADF) list, and a list of radio station frequencies for weather in one book. It's important to keep current on the weather when going around South Africa. The South African beacon system is excellent! All that is needed to go around South Africa are the relevant charts and a current light list so the beacons can be identified correctly.

Most boats carry a mixture of Defense Mapping Agency (DMA) and British Admiralty (BA) charts. When buying charts in the world, a person can generally find one or the other. To keep track of all the charts as a boat collection grows, it's useful to have both the DMA and BA chart catalogs on board. I started out with inventory from one source, DMA, but as time at sea progressed and as we visited new locations, we eventually ended up with both kinds on hand. Having both catalogs allowed us to index both types of charts and gave us an easy reference to either.

EAST LONDON, SOUTH AFRICA

December 15, 1992: We departed Durban with a calm. The barometer was at 1010 to 1011 millibars across the whole country. We motored on the one hundred-fathom curve in order to take advantage of the current.

December 16: An unexpected squall came in with a twenty-five knot wind from the southwest in the morning. The waves rapidly increased to a nine- to twelve-foot condition with a short, vertical chop, like boiling water. It was cool with a lot of rain. We beat to windward and stayed inside the one hundred-fathom curve, knowing that even if we made no progress to windward with the chop, we were still moving southwest with the two-knot current. Toward evening, the squall passed. However, it left a turbulent sea which gradually moderated. By midnight, the waves were down to a level where we could motor without going up and down so vertically on the chop that the prop came out of the water.

December 17: The turbulence of the waves continued to drop. We were able to make good progress by motor. The wind moved to the northeast at five knots. The waves were down to two feet, also from the northeast. There was a cloudy sky with eight-mile visibility. Our course was 227 degrees true with a 23 degree west variation. We were making seven and a half knots, measured by landmarks onshore using time and distance. We were now on the fifty-fathom curve, closing East London with a nice northeast sea breeze assisting us at ten knots. We arrived at East London at 1700 LT. There, we picked up fore and aft moorings up the river from the shipping docks.

East London is a good stop. But it's inconvenient to get provisions there unless a taxi is used. There is about a three-mile walk into town. In town, there is a great maritime museum where the Coelacanth is displayed. This is a fish, once thought to have been extinct for millions of years, until it was discovered alive in the thirties. It still lives in the depths of the Mozambique Channel.

PORT ELIZABETH, SOUTH AFRICA

December 21, 1992: We departed East London with light wind (five knots or less) and an overcast sky. A gale warning had been issued for Durban from the northeast with the possibility of it reaching East London. So, we slipped out ahead of it. We motored with the current assisting us.

December 22: The clouds cleared off in the morning and a five-knot, southwest wind came in. Later, the wind picked up to ten knots. We motor-sailed on the fifty-fathom curve directly for Port Elizabeth with a course of 277 degrees true. Along the way, we spotted our first cape seals. There were four of them.

We arrived at Port Elizabeth at 1800 LT and tied to the pier by the yacht club. Port Elizabeth is a pleasant harbor with a friendly yacht club. There's about a two-mile walk to town. An immigration office is there and we extended our visas.

December 25: What a great way we found to celebrate Christmas! We were en route around the cape. We departed Port Elizabeth at 0430 LT with a light, southeast wind. We wanted to get around the east point, going west, before the southeast wind picked up. Some sea lions were sleeping on the base of one of the channel buoys as we passed. Later, we saw several seals floating on their backs with their flippers straight up in the air like sails.

We enjoyed a beautiful night with the Magellan Clouds standing out well, and the Southern Cross was as beautiful as always. The wind was from the southeast at twenty-five knots. The waves were from six to nine feet.

December 26: The wind shifted to northeast at fifteen knots. The barometer dropped from 1018 to 1001 millibars. The wind shifted again to southwest at fifteen knots with a forecast of twenty-five knots, which didn't happen. With our course at 260 degrees true, we motor- sailed in order to get closer to the wind. The waves were from three to five feet. We followed the fifty-fathom curve.

December 27: The wind was southwest at fifteen knots and the waves were three to five feet. We motor-sailed around Cape Agulhas at 1900 LT.

HOUTS BAY, SOUTH AFRICA

December 28, 1992: We motor-sailed toward Houts Bay. The wind was southwest to west at ten knots or less and the waves were three feet. It was a very easy passage. Along the way, we saw seals, cape penguins, black ducks, cormorants, and a pair of albatross. The seals were very shy and stayed away from our boat.

We passed False Bay, which has embarrassed some navigators. Thinking they were clear of the Cape of Good Hope, they turned for the open sea to go up the coast, only to realize that they had turned too soon when they saw the end of the bay. Then, they had to beat back out of the bay and turn west northwest again in order to round the next point. Only then could they head up the west coast of Africa and into the Atlantic.

We passed Vasco da Gama Mountain. The famous Table Mountain sighted by so many captains over the centuries, stood out as well.

Happily, we entered Houts Bay. The high mountains on both sides of the bay reminded us of the Marquesas Islands, except that, here, there is a seal island with thousands of seals just north of the entrance to the bay. That's something not generally seen in the tropics where the Marquesas Islands are located.

Houts Bay is an excellent stop, especially before heading into the South Atlantic. It's about ten miles south of Cape Town. There is no problem clearing from Cape Town and departing from Houts Bay. The yacht club in Houts Bay is very nice. The harbor has floating piers for securing boats. There isn't the hassle of being in a big harbor. At the same time, there's the friendliness of a small town. There's also a good grocery store for getting provisioned for the trip across the Atlantic. We found all the prices in South Africa to be reasonable. Canned products were very good. They were all priced under three rand per can. Fresh cabbage was one rand per head.

The east South African coast has great, sand beaches for miles and miles with rolling grass hills, cliffs, and wooded ravines with creeks cascading to the ocean over small cliffs. Once past Port Elizabeth, the land becomes more mountainous. It flattens around Cape Agulhas, the southernmost point of land in Africa, and juts out high at Houts Bay and Table Mountain.

Our favorite stops in South Africa were the ones we had chosen for longer stays. These were Richards Bay, Durban, and Houts Bay.

While at Houts Bay, preparing for the last leg of our journey around the world, Marione and I thought of the many friends who had taken the Red Sea route in order to avoid going around the cape. How much tougher that route must be considering at least eight hundred miles of windward work. Add to that, having to contend with the heaviest shipping in the world, and then all the hassle of going through the Suez Canal. While they were pounding themselves, with mostly unfriendly shores on both sides, Marione and I were sitting in lovely Houts Bay anticipating a sail over the most beautiful sea conditions in the world. We were glad we had taken the route we did.

OUR SOUTH ATLANTIC PASSAGE

January 1,1993: With my visa for Brazil in hand, we departed Houts Bay at 0430 LT with a clear sky and a barometer reading of 1017 millibars. The wind was southwest at fifteen knots. Our course was 310 degrees true. We spotted four more seals and many types of birds, including petrels and boobies. Later in the day, the wind picked up to twenty knots. Around sunset, I could just make out Table Mountain, now some fifty miles behind us.

We planned to sail a curved route on our way to Natal, Brazil. We would go with the predominant trade wind and avoid the calm at the center of the South Atlantic high. This route would take us by St. Helena Island and Ascension Island.

January 2: The wind was south at fifteen to twenty knots and the waves were three to six feet from the south. We had a totally clear sky. Our position was 32 degrees 21 minutes south and 16 degrees 10 minutes east. The barometer read 1015 millibars. We saw many pintado petrels also called cape pigeons.

January 3: The wind was south southeast at twenty knots. The waves were three to six feet from the south southeast. We still had a beautiful, clear sky with the barometer at 1012 millibars. Later, the wind shifted to the south and fast-moving stratocumulus clouds began to move in from the south as well. ***Mermaid*** ran a port tack. There were many petrels again on this day.

January 4: The wind was south southwest to south at ten to twenty knots with waves of three feet and a swell of nine feet. The barometer was steady at 1012 millibars and there was a stratocumulus overcast with an occasional broken condition. There were black petrels around the boat.

January 5: The wind was variable from the south southeast to south southwest at fifteen knots. Under a clear sky, the water was a beautiful blue with small whitecaps. Later, the wind shifted to south southeast. Our position was 28 degrees 16 minutes south and 10 degrees 38 minutes east. At sunset, two killer whales, or orcas, swam by. One came up for air near the cockpit. Then, they swam away. After a bit, they returned, swimming under the stern and cockpit upside down, as if for a closer look. We could see their white undersides vividly as they swam very close to the bottom of the boat. These were the first orcas we had seen in our entire trip.

January 6: The wind was southeast at fifteen knots. The waves were southeast at three feet with a six-foot swell from the southwest (yes, southwest) and a clear sky. Fifteen pilot whales swam with us for about twenty minutes. They courteously gave ***Mermaid's*** hull sea room on the beam. We enjoyed a beautiful sailing day on the ***Mermaid*** with many more petrel flying around.

January 7: The sky went from clear in the morning to overcast, then back to clear once more, then to broken at sunset. The wind was east southeast at fifteen knots and the waves were three feet. Our position was 26 degrees 21 minutes south and 07 degrees 06 minutes east. Dolphins visited us today as did many more petrel.

January 8: The wind was east southeast at ten to fifteen knots. We passed through occasional showers under an overcast sky.

January 9: Again, there were stratus clouds and occasional showers. As we passed through a misty rain, the sun shone through the raindrops to put ***Mermaid*** in the center of a small rainbow. This beautiful experience caught our imaginations. It was as if we were passing through a mystical gateway to the completion of our circumnavigation. The wind seemed to carry us through, coming from the east southeast at ten to fifteen knots.

January 10: On this day, we sailed across the ***Tropic of Capricorn.*** The wind was southeast at ten knots. The sky was clear to seven-tenths broken. The waves were three feet from the southeast. Our position was 22 degrees 46 minutes south and 02 degrees 26 minutes east. We saw many birds.

January 11: The wind was fifteen knots from the southeast. The waves were three feet with an occasional six-foot swell. The day was marked by beautiful, clear, deep-blue water and flying fish. We crossed the ***sun's declination.*** The barometer stood at 1019 millibars.

January 12: There were rain showers. The wind was five knots or less. There was a seven-tenths broken cloud cover. We motored over a calm sea as we crossed back into the ***western hemisphere.*** A tropic bird flew over us, stopped above, and hovered, as if to greet us with a friendly, *"Hello!"*

January 13: Our course was 309 degrees true. Our position was 19 degrees 14 minutes south and 01 degree 19 minutes west. We motored with no wind in a calm sea, passing a small circuit-riding freighter. Starting its round in England, it services Ascension and Saint Helena Islands, then goes on to Cape Town, and then returns by the same route. Each round trip takes it about two months.

January 14: The calm continued with a small, long-interval swell. Many fish ran with ***Mermaid*** and jumped around the boat. Many birds also tagged along. The sky was clear. At sunset, we sighted a beautiful, green flash, almost like a camera flash bulb.

January 15: We motored in a flat calm with a horizon so hazy that I couldn't make it out at civil twilight (that time of day when you can see the horizon and the stars), in order to take a star shot. The ambiance was magical with stars reflecting in the water, fish jumping, and many flying fish sailing over the water's surface. There seems to be a prolific fish nursery in this region.

January 16: The wind was light to calm, although the wind tried to come back. We motor-sailed with tropic birds and other birds all around us. There were also many fish of all sizes jumping around the ***Mermaid***. Marione caught a jack. Unfortunately though, when it was filleted, the meat had worms in it. We sighted Saint Helena Island at sunset.

SAINT HELENA ISLAND

January 17, 1993: We arrived at Saint Helena Island before sunrise and heaved to until dawn. Then, we closed Jamestown, the only town on the island. St. Helena is a mountainous rock formation jutting out of the ocean, steep with cliffs all around. The anchorage at Jamestown is an open roadstead. As we approached, we could see the problems that would confront us on attempting a visit to Jamestown. A couple of yachts, anchored there in a five-foot swell, were doing the sideways, rolling jigaboo. The breakers were slamming the shore with all the power of the sea. If we landed here, we would then have to climb steps for a couple hundred feet just to arrive at the base of Jamestown since the town is built on a sloping hill. You might say that if you visit Jamestown, you are either climbing or trying to keep from falling down!

This island is where Napoleon was imprisoned by the British. With its high cliffs bordering the sea, it was like an impregnable fortress. I could imagine Napolean's feelings of hopelessness and frustration when he arrived at his new prison home.

It was Sunday when we arrived. Looking at that rough anchorage, and how difficult it would be to land, and beckoned by the wind picking up to fill our sails, Marione and I waved good-bye to St. Helena. We watched it pass over the horizon as we continued to sail in the most beautiful ocean in the world. The sky was clear and the wind blew up to ten knots from the southeast as we sailed away from St. Helena.

HOMING ON NATAL

January 18 And 19, 1993: The sky was clear to overacast and the wind was southeast at ten knots. The barometer was 1017 millibars.

January 20: The overcast in the morning cleared in the afternoon. The wind was southeast at ten knots. Our position was 12 degrees 31 minutes south and 09 degrees 24 minutes west.

January 21: No changes. A petrel slept aboard ***Mermaid*** all night.

January 22: The sky cleared in the morning. At noon and in the afternoon, we enjoyed sunshine. Then it became cloudy in the evening with showers at night. We sighted three frigate birds and many other types of birds.

We had a new experience which was a first for me. Some flying fish scattered on the surface of the water. A sailor sees this often, of course, but rarely does he see why they fly. This time we saw some fish in pursuit of the flying fish. The jacks jumped in and out of the water while watching the direction taken by the flying fish. The jacks moved as fast as the flying fish, even while jumping out of the water to track them. What a display of aggressiveness.

January 23: Conditions remained unchanged. The southeast wind continued at ten knots while the variability of cloud and sunshine followed the pattern of preceding days.

January 24: We sighted Ascension Island with its rocks and desolate terrain, just before sunset. By then, we were homing for Natal, Brazil, Marione's hometown. We decided to go on in our world of paradise and sailed right by Ascension Island, setting our course at 275 degrees true.

January 25: The wind was southeast at fifteen to twenty knots. At sunset, a huge battle-scarred orca with a six-foot dorsal fin came by ***Mermaid's*** stern, surfacing for air. It took a look at us and then swam away. Two noddy terns rode aboard overnight.

January 26: The wind was southeast at fifteen to twenty knots and the waves were five feet. We had perfect trade wind sailing conditions.

January 27: Sailing conditions remained the same. Five noddy terns rode with us overnight.

January 28: Sailing conditions remained unchanged. Our position was 07 degrees 49 minutes south and 20 degrees 16 minutes west. Eight noddy terns rode with us overnight. They were all riding on our awning. ***It looked like a chicken coop!*** I became concerned about the mess they might make on the awning. I decided if they were going to ride, it would be where I wanted them to be located. They were not at all frightened by my approach. I gently pushed them to where I wanted them to roost, at the side of the awning, hopefully with their business ends hanging over the side. They allowed me to move them. For the most part, they stayed where I put them.

January 29: The wind was more easterly in the morning, shifting back to southeast in the afternoon. We enjoyed some current assistance. The waves were a gentle three to five feet.

January 30: The wind was from the southeast at fifteen knots and the waves were three feet. What a beautiful sailing ocean we were enjoying! Our position was 07 degrees 33 minutes south and 23 degrees 20 minutes west. The noddy terns came in again just after sunset. I am certain that they were the same ones that had ridden with us before because they took up the same roosting spots. We hadn't seen them all day. They arrived at sunset, about sixty miles from where they had left us, rode the dark hours aboard, and left at dawn.

January 31: One noddy tern was aboard overnight. The wind was east to east southeast at ten to fifteen knots and there were three- to five-foot waves. There was scattered cumulus clouds. Our course was 277 degrees true and we had 21 degrees west variation. Many flying fish, jack, and other fish ran with us.

February 1: No change in the conditions. Seven noddy terns nested aboard overnight, apparently the same ones since they were in the same roosting spots.

February 2 and 3: Still no change in conditions. One noddy tern was aboard overnight. Five pilot whales swam by.

February 4: The wind was southeast at seven knots. The barometer read 1015 millibars. Our position was 06 degrees 20 minutes south and 30 degrees 36 minutes west. Three noddy terns from our little flock slept aboard. One left us a long, tail feather which I found in the cockpit in the morning. This feather wound up in the band of my straw hat. I wore it with pleasure, knowing it had come from a wild bird that had never been harmed by man and thus, had no fear of him.

February 5: A booby flew over in the morning and a tropic bird paid us a visit. The wind was east southeast at fifteen knots and the waves were three feet. The cloud cover was clear to broken. Our position was 06 degrees 06 minutes south and 32 degrees 09 minutes west.

HOME AT LAST: NATAL, BRAZIL

February 6, 1993: Two boobies visited us. There were more clouds and scattered showers. The wind was east southeast at fifteen to twenty knots, and stronger during the showers. We were closing Natal. As the sun set and twilight faded from the sky, the loom of Natal's lights stood bright on the stratus and stratocumulus clouds covering eight tenths of the sky.

It had been four years, almost to the day, since Marione and I had sailed from this shore. At the time, we could hardly talk to each other. Nevertheless, we were endowed with the universal language of love. Now as we sat in the cockpit watching the loom of Natal grow as we approached the city, we could communicate well. In contrast with the experience of our friends in Trinidad, where communication and understanding made their relationship less desirable, we found that communication had made our relationship richer and more rewarding.

Along the way, I had learned many interesting tidbits from Marione's youth. She grew up on a plantation ten miles from Natal. Her grandfather was one of her favorite relatives. He had lived to the ripe old age of ninety-four. His eyes were so deep blue that the Caribbean Sea reminded her of the color. She and her family had spent many hours listening to his great stories, drawn from his imagination and experiences.

When someone lives to be ninety-four, I always wonder what he did to stay alive so long. So, I asked Marione what he ate. At breakfast, he'd eat two fried eggs with meat, usually beef, and papa, chasing this with strong coffee. Papa is a thick mix of hot milk and the flour of mandioca. Mandioca is called casava in Spanish. However, this species is poisonous until the juice is squeezed out and the flour is dried. He made his coffee by putting four spoonfuls of coffee in a sock and pouring hot water through it. For lunch, he ate rice and beans, and chicken. He would drink cashew juice, made from the fruit of the cashew nut tree. He would finish this off with sliced mangoes. He ended the day with a light dinner of macaixiera, a non-poisonous casava, or sweet potato and more strong coffee. Mixed into his diet were coconuts, pineapple, and many other fruits and vegetables. He enjoyed smoking a pipe, using the tobacco leaf dried and rolled. He also chewed tobacco, but he did not drink. He worked hard all his life. His trade was that of a cowboy and rancher.

Admiring his friend's baby daughter one day, he said, *"When she grows up, I'm going to marry her!"*

And he did! They had nine children. He outlived her by four years.

When I met Marione, she had never used a washing machine or been to a Laundromat. I thought she'd be thrilled to be able to do laundry in such an easy way. Not so! The washing machine does not get the clothes as clean as hand washing. She prefers to wash clothes by hand. This is a bonus while traveling by sailboat. A good part of the world does laundry by hand. One can be hard pressed to find a washing machine in some places.

It seems that in this complex society of ours that instant self-gratification is its goal. The more we have, the more we expect, and the more it takes to please us. In its midst, I had found a lovely little lady, who is happy with very little: the fulfillment of looking at the stars or a flower, taking a shower with a bucket, eating a one-course meal, washing laundry by hand, and, in general, just being happy aboard the world of the ***Mermaid***.

The only thing that really matters to Marione is our relationship. Everything else is relative. It is wonderful to be down to the basics that really count and out of the self-imposed complexities. Yet, it is a good feeling to know that we have a choice and can step into the complexities if we so desire.

As Marione stood in the cockpit, with her lovely hair blowing in the wind and a look of maturity and beauty, excitedly anticipating landfall and the visit with her family, I realized how very fortunate I have been that fate had cast us together. Only a few minutes difference and our destiny would have been different. We might never have met.

Perhaps, it was meant to be. Marione had had a dream just the year before I met her. She had dreamed of a man coming from the sea on a boat, and of traveling around the world with him. It was a strange dream, as dreams are apt to be, particularly because, at the time, she had had nothing to do with the water or boats. She had never heard about a yacht club where boats might anchor. She told her mother about her dream. Her mother listened and then said it was only a dream.

I once asked her mother, *"Do you remember Marione telling you about her dream of a man coming from the sea?"*

"Yes I do! And that dream has come true!"

Was this a mystic experience foretelling Marione's future and mine? Or was it just the wishful dream of a young woman? In any case, it is strange that the man in her dream came from the sea at a time when the sea was not a part of her life. Ah, well! The sea is steeped in mystical occurrences. I may have one some day. Perhaps I already have.

February 7: Dawn was breaking. As civil twilight waned for another day, Marione's hometown was becoming visible in detail as we approached to close the port. ***It was great to return to Natal!*** It is a beautiful location with some of the finest beaches you can find. To appreciate Natal, you have to travel. When we returned to see the beauty of this place, we were both very happy to be back in the western hemisphere, back to North, Central, and South America, and the beautiful Caribbean Sea. This is the most beautiful part of the world in our opinions.

Natal is called *"The Sun City"* with its beautiful sand beaches and great sand dunes. Average temperatures are always in the 70- to 80-degree F range, and there are no hurricanes! During World War II, Natal was also called the *"Diving Board to Victory"* by the allies. All the airplanes heading for the North

African campaign left from here. Indeed, the yacht club was the American Officers Club in those days.

Marione once told me a story she had heard that took place here in World War II at the officers club. It took place on the Yankee Thanksgiving. ***The menu at the officers club always had turkey*** on it. On the Yankee Thanksgiving Day, there wasn't enough turkey to go around. So, a substitution was made without informing the Yanks. Vulture was served, since that bird was plentiful. The Yanks ate it, believing it to be turkey.

Later, when thcy were asked how it was, they replied, *"It was good, but a little tough!"*

Thank goodness for the Yanks, a friendly, energetic, forgiving, and when necessary, very tough people!

The wind was east southeast at fifteen to twenty knots with showers, as we closed the channel to Natal. The Natal channel leads into a river, with a reef on either side of the channel entrance. There is a prevailing wind when closing the channel. This means a running sea (waves pushing from astern) and a wind blowing you toward shore.

I intended to close with sail, but started my motor for backup, following my usual procedure, described before, using as many of my three approach options (sail, motor, and anchor) as possible. Here, all three were available.

With sails up and the motor on, we approached the channel. About one hundred feet from the channel entrance, the engine transmission stopped! There was no need to worry. We could sail in. Fortunately, we arrived in a high slack tide and, so, did not have a fast outflow current problem from the river. We sailed up to the yacht club and anchored.

Had we depended exclusively on the motor with no sail option, it might have turned out badly for us and ***Mermaid***. When the engine failed at such a critical time, there would have been little time left for raising the sails. Alternately, anchoring would probably have left little room for scope in front of the reef. What was really not an emergency could have turned into one without proper backup planning.

Marione's dad was very happy to see her. He was down to greet us within fifteen minutes of our arrival. The last time he had seen Marione, she had been twenty-four years old and hardly ever out of the house. Now, he was looking at a strong, beautiful woman who had just sailed around the world!

While waiting to clear immigration at the Natal Yacht Club, we also saw Zeca and his wife, Lucia. Zeca is the fellow who had done the interpreting for me in my first meeting with Marione's father. As a result of that experience, the four of us had a kindred relationship and enjoyed a friendly chat.

Once we had cleared in, we were off to see the rest of Marione's family. We were loaded down with the presents we'd purchased for them in various ports. I do believe ***Mermaid*** raised a couple of inches on her waterline when we unloaded the gifts. Doing so was a pleasant reminder of how big ***Mermaid*** had been before we loaded so much aboard. Marione and her family had a wonderful reunion catching up on each others activities. We were all enjoying the visit. My thoughts, nevertheless, turned to the repair of the transmission.

Once back on the ***Mermaid***, to my great relief, on disconnecting the transmission from the engine, I quickly located the problem. Rather than looking at rebuilding the transmission, ***if I was lucky***, I simply needed to replace the shock coupling that connects the engine to the transmission. I thought, *"This should be easy to fix. All I need is the part."* It turned out not to be as simple as I had imagined. The transmission was a Borg Warner. I went to the local Borg Warner distributor. He didn't have the part. When he called Sao Paulo, nobody there had the part or knew where one could be obtained. So, I got a telephone number out of my manual and called Borg Warner in the United States. They gave me a number for the marine division. I called the marine division to ask where I could buy the coupling in Brazil. It was not available in Brazil. The nearest distributor was in Argentina.

It seemed I would have better luck if I ordered the part from the United States. So I called to order the part after getting the name of the distributor in Ft. Lauderdale, Florida. The part cost twenty-six dollars. I ordered two just in case my transmission had a bigger problem. They shipped me two parts with three-day service. Then it took two more weeks to get it out of Brazilian Customs. I was thrilled when I finally got the parts. On opening the box, I beheld the shiny new parts, each with a stamp in the steel saying, ***"Made in Brazil."*** Well, there has to be a bright side to every story! The bright side of this one is that customs did not charge any import duty.

We had a most enjoyable, warm, and friendly visit in Brazil with Marione's family and many old friends. By now it was April 15, 1993. I wanted to get across the Caribbean before hurricane season. Marione and I could both hear the beckoning of the lovely South Atlantic calling. This happens when you have been to sea a long time. The sea becomes part of you. When you live in it below deck and only four feet above it the rest of the time, you become as salty as the sea and a part of it. It was time for us to leave.

We bid our farewells. I know it is difficult for Marione's family to understand why anyone would want to live on the sea and not be around the family all the time. But my little woman had become as much of an adventurer as I. She, too, felt the call of the beautiful, rolling sea with its vastness and peace, of living with nature in all her moods, and of the living sea.

April 18, 1993: ***We raised the anchor*** and motor-sailed out the channel with all three options in hand, into a beautiful east southeast trade wind. We stowed the anchor, secured the motor, and let the South Atlantic envelope us into its vastness and overwhelming beauty.

As we sailed into the tranquillity of the sea, Marione slipped her hand in mine and told me, *"You are my prince, my wonderful man, and the man of my dreams. I love you very much!"*

As I love my Marione.

HOPE

There was a glimmer
That sparked a simmer
In the inner of a few men.
Their names were John, George, and Tom,
Pierre, Lafayette, and Ben
And more then one can pen.
They had a dream and made it seem
There was hope for all of them.

Perhaps there was, perhaps there is
And thank goodness the flag they flew
Is my flag colored red, white and blue.
The Stars and Stripes, the Union Jack
and the French flag too

Of many lands there are but a few
Where dreamers can proclaim the hope for man.
If these lands don't take a stand
There is little hope for modern man
And it will assure the survival
Of narrow views and ignorance at hand.

APPENDIX ONE
NAVIGATION

The stars are forever and the sun and planets
The electronics are but a fortnight
And one can never know when they'll quit
But only that they will quit
And generally at the wrong time.

MY FAVORITE PUBLICATIONS FOR NAVIGATION

1. ***Ocean Planning Guides*** published for each ocean by the Defense Mapping Agency.
2. ***Sailing Directions En Route*** published by the Defense Mapping Agency.
3. ***Privately Written Cruising Guides*** for areas you plan to cruise extensively.
4. ***Sight Reduction Tables*** (H.O. PUB NO. 249, Volumes I, II, III) published by the Defense Mapping Agency.
5. ***Nautical Almanac*** issued by the United States Naval Observatory.
6. ***World Port Index*** published by the Defense Mapping Agency.
7. ***Worldwide Marine Weather Broadcasts*** sold by the U.S. Government Printing Office.
8. ***Travel Information Manual (TIM).*** You can get an old copy from your travel agent, airline, or fax 02503-73515 in the Netherlands. It is published monthly, but you only need one copy every couple years. It contains visa, pet, and vaccination requirements for each country worldwide, and also shows disease epidemic areas.
9. ***Charts***-Carry Defense Mapping Agency catalogs and the British Admiralty charts catalog. One or the other or both kinds of charts are fine.
10. ***Light List***-When cruising it is generally never current.
11. ***Tide Table***-Generally expires en route and needs updating. Your Ocean Planning Guide will also give you area tidal range.

APPENDIX II
NICE FEATURES ON A CRUISING BOAT:

1. The capability to raise and lower your mast without shore assistance.
2. An engine drive shaft assembly slightly offset from the rudder post so it can be removed slipping past the rudder.
3. A stuffing box with easy access to check and adjust.
4. All seacocks having easy access to turn on and off.
5. A comfortable helm chair in the cockpit.
6. An adjustable cockpit awning to prevent sun and water glare from morning and afternoon sunshine.
7. A securely mounted compass you can take bearings across the top of and hold onto.
8. A protected propeller, as one in a horn timber, to help prevent tangle in nets and rope.
9. A bottom shape that is easy to careen.
10. Not over a six-foot draft because it restricts gunk-holing too much.
11. A main sail with three sets of reef points.
12. A hard hull, sailing and motoring dinghy with good flotation.
13. Steps on the mast to the top.
14. An aluminum propane tank.
15. A diesel fuel tank with a bottom drain sump. This way you can run off dirt and water.
16. A removable drip pan under the engine.
17. No shower water to the bilge. Use a holding tank and pump.
18. The capability to drain the engine oil from the oil pan, under the engine, when changing oil.
19. Deck prisms for below deck lighting and fewer portholes can make more room for below deck storage and more privacy.
20. The hull and deck painted white. This will make a cooler boat in the tropics.

APPENDIX III

CAUTION:

A safety harness can be an illusion of safety if the line is too long or if you hook it on the stanchion line at the rail of your boat. The line must be short enough to prevent you from falling off the deck A line that allows you to dangle over the side or fall into the water could drown you. For real security, run a line down the ***center*** of your boat and hook a ***short safety line*** from your harness to that line. When you have your safety line stretched to full length be sure it stops you at the life line at the rail.

Here is my case in point. Just recently off Florida, the coast guard boarded a sailing vessel underway being steered by the automatic pilot. The skipper was dragging on his long rope harness in the water and he had drowned.

A few years ago in Vancouver, I remember a sailor with his inexperienced wife aboard. They were sailing with an automatic pilot. He had a long line harness on and fell overboard, catching his foot in the harness rope. He was being dragged in the water by the boat, foot first, as his wife panicked, jumping up and down screaming. A passing motorboat skipper saw the situation and raced over, boarding the sailboat and stopping it. But by then the skipper had drowned.